Check, Please!

ALSO BY JANICE DICKINSON

Everything About Me Is Fake . . . And I'm Perfect!

No Lifeguard on Duty

Check, Please!

Dating, Mating, & Extricating

JANICE DICKINSON

HC

An Imprint of HarperCollins*Publishers*

Photographs by Mathū Andersen.

A hardcover edition of this book was published in 2006 by HarperCollins Publishers.

HarperCollins books may be purchased for educational, business, or sales promotional use. For information please write: Special Markets Department, HarperCollins Publishers Inc., 10 East 53rd Street, New York, NY 10022.

FIRST PAPERBACK EDITION PUBLISHED 2007.

Designed by Kris Tobiassen

The Library of Congress has cataloged the hardcover edition as follows:

Dickinson, Janice, 1955–
    Check, please! : Dating, Mating, and Extricating / Janice
Dickinson.—1st ed.
        p. cm.
    Includes index.
    ISBN 0-06-076391-4 (alk. paper)
    ISBN13: 978-0-06-076391-6
    1. Dating (Social customs) 2. Man-woman relationships. 3. Mate selection. I. Title.

    HQ801.D532 2006
    306.73082'0973—dc22

                                                            2005057596

ISBN 13: 978-0-06-083433-3 (pbk.)
ISBN 10: 0-06-083433-1 (pbk.)

07   08   09   10   11   WBC/RRD   10 9 8 7 6 5 4 3 2 1

*To my infallibly phenomenal shining star who, on a daily basis,
exudes perfection extraordinaire. All of my love,
Savvy, all of my love.*

*To the love of my life, Nathan my son my son, who was the first
on the horizon of brilliance that made everything just right.
Rock 'em hard always!*

*To Brian, my search for contentment ended the moment you
called my bluff and filled my soul with love, laughter, and love.
You are the very reason for oxygen, now and forever;
my search is now over, more than ever.*

Love, Janice

We're too young to reason
Too grown up to dream
Now spring is turning
Your face to mine
I can hear your laughter
I can see your smile
No I can't escape
I'm a slave to love

—BRYAN FERRY,
"SLAVE TO LOVE"

CONTENTS

Part I: Dating

Part II: Advanced Dating Techniques

Part III: Mating

Part IV: Extricating

FOREWORD

By Jon Lovitz

MR. CHOW IN NEW YORK CITY

A busy evening at Mr. Chow restaurant, 7:30 P.M. An interviewer from the New Yorker *sits at a table, by himself.*

INTERVIEWER (V.O.): I sat at the table by myself, awaiting the arrival of the world's first supermodel, Janice Dickinson. I was fifteen minutes early. Mr. Chow was full of the usual celebrities, wannabe celebrities, actors and actresses, writers, even Donald Trump himself. Everybody was very excited to see and be seen. The noise level was fairly high. At exactly 7:30 P.M., on the dot, I heard a woman's voice yell through the cacophony, "I'm here! We can all eat now!" Donald Trump rose to his feet to meet the tall, tan brunette with the figure of a, well, supermodel. She stopped at at least six tables, blowing air kisses (so as not to mess up her makeup), and receiving congratulations on her new book (her second, by the way) *Everything About Me Is Fake . . . and I'm Perfect* before reaching my table. And, yes, she looked not just perfect, but beautiful, at least fifteen years younger than her admitted age. And she had the energy of an eighteen-year-old track star. "We love you, Janice!" was an oft-repeated refrain, to which she would re-spond, "Of course! What's not to love?" Indeed, Janice Dickinson had arrived.

JANICE DICKINSON (SITTING DOWN): Sorry I'm late.

INTERVIEWER: Don't be silly. You're exactly on time.

JANICE DICKINSON: Good! I'm a freak about being punctual. I hate being late. I wish I could be more relaxed about it, like my best friend, Jon Lovitz. He's always late. But he's so damned sexy, I for-give him.

INTERVIEWER: Wait a second. Jon Lovitz is your best friend? And he's sexy?

JANICE DICKINSON: Oh, yeah, baby. He's hot. Believe me, I know everybody and he's got it going on. In fact, I was just with him at the World Series.

INTERVIEWER: You're a baseball fan?

JANICE DICKINSON: Are you fucking kidding me? I love baseball. I'd marry a bat and take it home with me every night if I could.

INTERVIEWER: What's stopping you?

JANICE DICKINSON: I have an eleven-year-old daughter. I'm a PTA mother now. It's too hard to explain to a ten-year-old why Mommy's new boyfriend is a three-foot-long, round piece of lumber. Anyway, the game was fantastic. Did you catch it on TV?

INTERVIEWER: No. Tell me about it.

JANICE DICKINSON: Well, it was only possibly the greatest game in the history of the World Series. It came down to the bottom of the ninth inning, bases loaded, two outs. Barry Bonds is at the plate. A grand slam would not only win the series, but give him the all-time home run record in baseball. People were just going fucking nuts.

INTERVIEWER: I can imagine.

JANICE DICKINSON: Yeah, I had on these Dolce & Gabbana fuck-me pumps, a miniskirt slit up to here, my fake tits were popping out of my Calvin Klein mini-tee, and my Harry Winston earrings on loan were so goddamned big, it was all I could do to hold my head up. So everyone's watching Barry, and of course I'm thinking, "How hot do I look right now? Why isn't anyone staring at me?" So I stand up right as the pitcher hurls a hundred-mile-an-hour fastball toward the plate. And as I stand up, my left earring catches the sun and the glare lands right on Barry Bonds's face. I mean, right in his big, brown African American eyes. And he closes them, and the next thing you know, the ball hits him on the head. So he rushes the mound, tackles the pitcher, the benches on both teams empty, and there's a huge, full-scale brawl on the field. Then a fight breaks out in the stands; suddenly, there's a world-class riot. I said, "Lovitz, get me the fuck out of here, now, before some drunk moron decides to lob his beer can and pop one of my newly ac-quired Dr. Frank Ryan tits."

INTERVIEWER: What happened?

JANICE DICKINSON: Jon Lovitz is nice. But he's got to be one of the slowest people I've ever met. He starts whining about how he wants to see the end of the game. So I yank him up by his shirt and we haul ass out of there.

INTERVIEWER: So how did the game end?

JANICE DICKINSON: Fuck the game. How about my new tits?

INTERVIEWER: They're very nice.

JANICE DICKINSON: Really? They're not too small?

INTERVIEWER: No, they're perfect.

JANICE DICKINSON: You should see my legs. They're even better.

INTERVIEWER: Let's talk about your book.

JANICE DICKINSON: Yeah, let's. Did you ever bother to fucking read it?

INTERVIEWER: Yes, I liked it very much.

JANICE DICKINSON: Oh . . . but you didn't *love* it? Well, why don't I just take all ten zillion advance orders, put them in a pile, douse them with kerosene, and have a book-burning party?

INTERVIEWER: No, I think you misunderstood me. I really liked your book.

JANICE DICKINSON: I know. But I want people to *love* it. Sorry—I have rage issues. Where's that Chinese waiter of ours? I'm so fucking hungry, I'll eat his dog if he doesn't bring me a spring dumpling or some seaweed, which, by the way, is good for your complexion. (*calling to a waiter*) Hey, you! Chow boy! Yeah, you, come here!

WAITER: Yes, miss?

JANICE DICKINSON: Yeah, I'm sorry to bother you. What's your name?

WAITER: Joe.

JANICE DICKINSON: Joe? You look Chinese.

WAITER: I am.

JANICE DICKINSON: Oh, well, good for you. I love the Chinese. I hope I didn't offend you. You know, I may be part Chinese myself. You can tell by my eyes and my nipples. Listen, where are you going with that food?

WAITER: It's for Mr. Trump.

JANICE DICKINSON: Look, could you just let me have it? With my anger issues, if I don't eat something right now, I'm liable to strut on over to the Donald, wrap my perfectly yoga-toned legs around his face, and rip that toupee right off his head!

INTERVIEWER: I think that's his real hair.

JANICE DICKINSON: Yeah, and these are my real tits. Come on. Just put the food here and tell him the world's first supermodel insisted you give it to her. He'll love it, he's a fucking billionaire, for Chrissake. They're all the same.

The waiter puts down the five plates of food at Janice's table and leaves.

INTERVIEWER: That's amazing.

JANICE DICKINSON: Oh, please. That waiter was ready to dive down my dress and have at me with his chopsticks. He probably thinks my pussy is sushi.
    You know, I have a sweet side.

INTERVIEWER: I'm sure you do.

JANICE DICKINSON: No one ever talks about it. I'm a completely different person around my daughter.

INTERVIEWER: So I understand you're working on a third book?

JANICE DICKINSON: Yes, it will be a woman's guide to dating. It's called *Check, Please!*

WAITER: Yes, Miss Dickinson, coming right away.

JANICE DICKINSON: No, that's the name of the book. Maybe I should change it. How about *If It Moves . . .*

INTERVIEWER: So it's about dating?

JANICE DICKINSON: Yes. What to do, what not to do. How to dress, how to do your makeup, hair, walk, make love, the whole thing. And some of the great dates I've had and some of the horrible ones.

INTERVIEWER: Tell me about a bad one.

JANICE DICKINSON: Well, I don't like to name names, but—

INTERVIEWER: You don't?

JANICE DICKINSON: Not anymore. I did enough of that in the first book. In the second book I trashed Russell Simmons's wife and got my wrists slapped, so I'm being more careful in the new one.

INTERVIEWER: I understand.

JANICE DICKINSON: So get this. Just last week, I get invited to go on a date. I've met the guy once before. He's really rich, really famous, but who cares, because he's got horrendous breath. I said, "Hey, Buddy, I'd like to go out with you, but I'm afraid your breath might melt my new Dr. Ryan cheek and buttocks implants."

INTERVIEWER: You had a butt implant?

JANICE DICKINSON: Honey, I've had everything. My nails are acrylic, my eyebrows are tattooed, my breasts are silicone, then saline, my face is BOTOX. But who gives a shit? At least I'm honest about it.

INTERVIEWER: What about your lips?

JANICE DICKINSON: The lips are all mine, baby. They're what make me one sexy bitch. That's the name of my new perfume: *Sexy Bitch!* That's me! Anyway, I turn this guy down. And then he tells me he's got floor seats to the Lakers playoff game. I said, "I've got Listerine strips in my purse. Pick me up at seven, Denzel."

INTERVIEWER: Denzel Washington?

JANICE DICKINSON: Oh shit, did I say that? Ah, fuck it, it's just one more mad self-absorbed asshole. So, I'm sitting on the floor at the game—

INTERVIEWER: Floor seats? That must have been exciting.

JANICE DICKINSON: Are you kidding? My date's breath was so bad, I had to keep turning my head and talking to some blond bimbo who kept asking me for fashion tips. And trust me, they wouldn't have helped.

INTERVIEWER: But was it really Denzel—

JANICE DICKINSON: Fuck Denzel! I was there to see Yao Ming! Yeah, baby, give me a few yards of that seven-foot-six Chinese manhood!!!

INTERVIEWER: Check, please!

The End

ACKNOWLEDGMENTS

Thanks to my editor, Cal Morgan—the greatest, period—and his lovely wife, Cassie. God knows how you do it! To Judith Regan, the Jagermeister herself, the omnipotent. You alpha female, you! To Miss Elizabeth Yarborough, thank you from the bottom of heart. I couldn't have done this without you. My friends at UTA, especially Lee Horvitz, Hayden Meyer, Jonathan Swaden, Anne Bartnett, Karrie Wolfe, Jacob Senton, and Jessica Weiner—thank you, thank you, thank you, thank you, thank you all. Marc Kesten, Esq., attorney of attorneys, and his amazing son, Duke. My fabulously gaudy West Coast publicist, Avo Yermagyan of Gaudy PR . . . You're in the army now! Mathū Andersen, thank you for your genius, wit, and talent. Gabrial Geismar: The part of my brain that *Vogue* lobotomized, you restore monthly. Thanks for your endless humor, style, and fierceness. Duke Snyder, you are the "Rock Star of Hair," period. The best, best, best executive producer ever, Stuart Krasnow! Thank you for the *Janice Dickinson Modeling Agency*. We will rule the world! And thanks to his better half, Freddy. To Kevin Williams, Garret Jacobs, and Damon Lewis, thank you all from the bottom of my heart. Alice Dickens and the rest of my family at Oxygen Network, You rock! My director, Darren Ewing, you rock! Jon Lovitz, the hottest, the sex symbol icon, the megalicious babe, the true leading man of leading men, thank you for our friendship. Dodd Mitchell, design genius extraordinaire, for endless laughs and rockin' my socks off. Jesse Metcalf, even though I don't have a pool! The glorious Miss Tyra Banks, you're the greatest! Mr. Ken Mock, thank you. My friends at *America's Next Top Model*: Anthony Domenici, Dana Gabrion, Larry Baron: Don Ostroff, and Les Moonves at CBS. My great friend Nora Laller. Thanks for my birthday party. VH1. Mimi and Maggie, thanks! The whole *Surreal Life* crew. Alexis and Mitch Mayor, my love and thanks! Debbie and Evan Dickinson, my love and thanks! Michael Birnbaum and Andrea Parker for relentless patience on the mountaintop end. Linda Michaels, the best grandmother. Joel and Eileen Birnbaum, you are the greatest grandparents from San Francisco to New York. Bill and Jackie, at Elite Los Angeles. Douglas and Monique Pillard, at Elite New York. Brian Bantree Agency, special thanks to Kirsten for managing the affairs of my life. Charlie Braka. You, your photos, and your makeup—everything about you rocks. Andre, the trainer of trainers, all my love. Joey Santos, chef of chefs, the best I've ever tasted! Brian Alexik, thank you for your generosity. Robert Sumrell, the best set designer to exist! Robert McDonald, who trims my roots like no other! Damon Vince King and your sidekick Calvin, I love your endless not-funny humor. Doreen, my horny travel agent gal! Jerome Terry, a true god of hair, *merci* and major heaps of gratitude forever! And thanks to the gang at the Jerome Terry Salon, especially June Bug and Larry. Anyone who has slept with Elvis deserves my respect, you bitch! Thank you to all of my neighbors, except for the drunk next door! Pete, we miss you, come back! To all the butchers, bakers, and candlestick makers at Beverly Glen Market. To the Beverly Glen Cleaners, for the wonderful dry-cleaning of all my party dresses. The entire Beverly Glen Deli, thank you. The Beverly Glen Pharmacy, especially Sue and Marc. Thanks for all the drugs! Hugo Christenson, thank you. The Raleigh Hotel, Miami Beach. Hugo Yanes and Susan Yenni and the Royalton Hotel. To Matt Rettenmund for your tireless, relentless humanitarianism and generosity. Without you, I'm nothing.

Elizabeth Tracy and her loving husband, Chuck Meyer, thanks for everything! Erika Peyton, Ms. Jonda, Coach Keith—you're the greatest. Yorlenny from the Warner Sports Program, thank you. Principal Kaufmann, keep up the good work. Vicki Feldmar, thank you. Ms. Sperling, and all of you from the Warner Star Program; you rock. The Rosa family, my many thanks! Joe and Jules Watson, thank you. Tommy Frye and his Brother Matt. I'm over the moon about you guys. The gang from the Snake Pit, you rock! The Haskell family, thank you. The entire Thacker family. Mark McVeigh, thank you. Paige Jenkins, thank you. Bruce Weber, thank you. Jan Stern, thanks for all of your help. Uzzi, Yael, and Ettai and Jacob Reiss, thank you, thank you, thank you. . . . To Dolce & Gabbana, Marc Jacobs, Christian Louboutin, Valentino, Judith Ripka—especially Brian Ripka, Fendi, Chopard, Heatherette—Richie Rich and Traver Rains, Film Fashion, and the list goes on, and on, and on. . . .

CONSUMER WARNING!

If you bought this book looking for a portable shoulder to cry on, or a literary big sis who'll be there to tell you over and over again, "Hey, you're doing everything right—it's the guys who need help!" . . . well, what can I say but: Wrong.

Check, Please! is a big dose of reality for those of you actually living the "surreal life" of dating, mating, and extricating. It'll help you, I promise—but I mean help you the Janice way. I'm no hand-holder. I'm gnarly. I'm all about tough love. So open your mind and let's rearrange the rules to help make you America's next top guy magnet.

Introduction

Those Who Cannot Learn from ~~History~~ . . . Her

AN ORACLE IS BORN

I was at my daughter's soccer game. Right away, I spotted a hot single daddy I've flirted with forever. We'll get into him later—or, if he's lucky, he'll get into me.

Let's call him Soccer Dad.

At the game, this macho, sexy Soccer Dad had a date who was depressing the hell out of me. She was a young, fresh, red-headed bombshell who seemed nice. Why did she have to be nice when I wanted to hate her?

Red Riding Hood said to me, "I love your books. Are they bestsellers? Are you still on TV?" She wasn't being a bitch—she just lived under a rock.

I said, "Thanks. My books *are* bestsellers and I'm *always* on TV. Plus, I'm currently working on a dating book."

This sexy woman, with a guy I'd like to mack any day of the week, looked sadly at her Jimmy Choos when her man wasn't listening and whispered to me, "Doesn't dating suck?"

"*My* dates don't think so," I shot back. "And when I think a date sucks, I just turn to the guy and say, 'Check, please!' He doesn't have to be a former waiter to know what *that* means."

She smiled. And in that moment it dawned on me that this was why I was writing this book—about the lessons I've learned and rules I've reinvented during my life's search for contentment. This book is my calling.

You may be thinking, "Who the fuck does she think she is? How can the world's first supermodel, who's been married and divorced three times and hooked up with famous Casanovas like Bruce Willis, Mick Jagger, Warren Beatty, and Sly Stallone, be any kind of oracle when it comes to men?"

Oh, wait—you just answered your own question.

Sure, I've absolutely been through some dating experiences that *have* sucked. But I'm writing this book because over the years I've dated some of the most interesting men on the planet and have been on some pretty amazing dates. I've done my best to have fun with them, and make sure the experience didn't suck for the guy or for me. Dating can actually rock if you're an achiever in life.

The sex ain't half bad, either.

See, the truth is, even though my last book was called *Everything About Me Is Fake . . . And I'm Perfect,* when it comes to guys I'm the first to admit I'm far from perfect. Am I really an oracle? Well, let's just say I know exactly what to do in any given situation—but as far as following my own advice . . . *fuhgeddaboudit!*

But that's the point. My imperfect past makes me the perfect guide for all my homegirls, because I've seen it all and done them—I mean *it*—all. I need an accounting firm to figure out how many dates I've been on! (An accounting firm. I like the sound of Earnest & Young. Oh, wait . . .)

Every chick is different, but you'll find all the basics you need to survive dating and mating in this book, including the fundamentals, like creating rules and having boundaries. You'll also pick up some good advice on how to extricate yourself from any pointless, or harmful, or un-fun situation.

My goal is to arrange it so that you'll never look at men the same way again—because unless you're 100 percent satisfied with your dating track record, you probably shouldn't anyway.

Get ready—this is going to be a little like a live feed.

THE WORST DATE I'VE EVER HAD—BAR NONE

Don't worry—bad dates are more fun to read about than they are to be on. This story will demonstrate how important it is to know the score before you go on even one more date.

Not *so* many years ago, when I was on the cover of a little fashion magazine called *Vogue*, I got a call from a hairdresser named Ara Gallant, inviting me to his place for a bash.

Ara had done that famous chopped look on Twiggy in the sixties and if it weren't for him I never would've made it *into* American *Vogue*, never mind landing on the cover. It was Ara who'd seen my portfolio when I was in the late, great Richard Avedon's studio, interviewing for work.

"You must shoot her," Ara told Avedon, the world's most famous photographer.

While that was being decided, I buddied up with Ara, who began inviting me to his Upper East Side apartment at night for little social get-togethers with the rich and infamous. Any night you were there you'd run into a grab bag of glitterati. One night, I talked movies with a short young rake everyone said would be ultrafamous someday.

His name? Jack Nicholson.

Another night, a little guy was coming on to me in the worst way, but I just never found Dustin Hoffman to be that fucking attractive. Mick Jagger would wander in and toss me his best lusty gaze. Of course, if you read my first book, *No Lifeguard on Duty*, you know that eventually wound up working on me. I once went up to Candice Bergen and said, "You're so beautiful." She turned to me and said, "Shut up."

A party at Ara's pad was like the original *Surreal Life*. What I remember most about his parties isn't the sexy men and chic women, but the surroundings: The apartment's walls were as black as Andy Warhol's Factory walls were silver, and all the furniture was fluorescent. You didn't even have to be high to feel high. But chances are that you were high anyway—the only thing more over the top than the guest list was the array of illicit party favors. More drugs than a Colombian pharmacy.

I, of course, accepted his latest invitation and showed up looking hot and ready for anything that came my way. I was, too.

I was trying my best to fend off Mick (this was back when I was still playing hard to get with him) when my host asked to speak to me in private. Sounded serious.

"Roman wants to meet you," Ara said, like I should be blown away.

"Who the fuck is Roman? I'm not into Italians." So sue me: I was still a mostly innocent twenty-year-old.

"Roman *Polanski,* Janice. The director—you know, *Rosemary's Baby. Chinatown.* He could be a great help to you," said Ara always looking out for my career.

My ears pricked up at that. I remembered seeing an article in the *New York Times* about a hotshot young director who was changing Hollywood. Of course, once I cleared my brain a bit from the evening's activities, I realized that this was also the man whose pregnant wife, the fabulous, glamorous Sharon Tate, had been butchered by that psycho Charles Manson. I was up on my world affairs.

"Oh, *that* Roman," I replied smoothly to Ara. I was thinking that maybe a dose of Roman Polanski was exactly what I needed. I'd help this guy heal, and he'd serve as my boyfriend and creative mentor.

I met him briefly and a date was set. It was a done deal.

(Now, just to be clear—this was a few years *before* he pled guilty to having sex with thirteen-year-old aspiring model at his buddy Jack Nicholson's house. I don't normally recommend self-confessed felons as good date material. Before he had to flee the country to avoid serving time in prison, the Roman Polanski brand was nothing more than a tragic, creative genius filled with promise. But if he wasn't notorious yet, he was also a bit of a mystery.)

For now, I was looking forward to this little *tête-à-tête* with the bad-boy director. So I took the little money I had in the bank and splurged on a $500 Gucci dress. I considered it an investment in my future.

As I would soon discover, Roman Polanski was a riddle inside a mystery wrapped in an enigma trapped in the body of a sex dwarf.

He took me to a play in Manhattan. Good start—I'll give him that. It's only when they take you to a musical that you need to start wondering if they have a secret boyfriend stashed somewhere.

It all seemed so romantic and filled with promise—beauty and the brain. He could make me a star! He would be my creative mentor and I'd be his muse. We'd be the Arthur Miller and Marilyn Monroe of the seventies, right? Right?

Wrong.

For most of our date, the man spoke not a word to me. Blind date, good; *mute* date, bad. He just sat there as if he were in some sort of daze. Before long I was wondering if I should check his pulse; maybe the little dude had lapsed into a coma. I knew *I* was in danger of lapsing into unconsciousness, I was so fucking bored.

I do remember wondering, at some point that night, "Is he still thinking about his wife's murder?" Classic mistake: The minute you start giving men credit for being deep, you're entering the realm of the imagination.

Finally, in the car on the way to dinner, he spoke.

"So, are we going to be having sex tonight?" he asked me in that thick Polish accent of his. He did it just like that—blatant little bastard. The word *proposition* is too classy for this kind of crude question.

I ignored him. He found his inner manners and rephrased the question.

"Shall we have sex this evening?" he posed. Somehow, hearing it asked more elegantly made it sound even dirtier.

I didn't answer him.

Roman then took me to dinner at the in spot of the moment: Elaine's on the Upper East Side, one of his favorite places.

Finally, over dessert (he ate it, I ogled it), he came up with a different conversation topic.

"Can you act?" he asked.

What do you think I'm doing right now? I thought. *I'm acting like I'm enjoying this date.*

Even back then, though, I knew this much: With any man you meet, you have to consider the entire package. It's a hard-and-fast dating rule. In the plus column, the guy had talent and connections. He may have been one of the most visionary directors in Hollywood history. Still, if he couldn't see that his behavior made him the most boring and rudest human alive, if he couldn't see that he was making the hot young babe across from him miserable, he was pretty much a blind date after all.

So I blew off his question about acting, even though I knew I was probably throwing away my big shot at being the next Mia Farrow or Faye Dunaway.

After Elaine's, he decided to try me one more time.

"Are you fucking me tonight?" he demanded.

By now, I'd had it. "Roman, I wouldn't touch you with a ten-foot pole." That must have hurt: After all, he was only a five-and-a-half-foot Pole. We went straight back to silence.

When it was all over, we got into his limo and he dropped me off without saying another word. Not one syllable. Phil Spector is probably a better date than Roman Polanski.

The point is, I was too young to know that I could have called for the check at any point during the disastrous date. That's one thing you've got to learn early, and remember often, girls: You can call for the check anytime, anyplace, and on anyone—even on the rich and infamous.

It was a good lesson. I didn't need to sleep with a disgusting vermin, pond-scum pig of a human being—the kind who probably wouldn't talk to you after he fucked you—to score a part. I didn't need to date men who were so limited in their intentions. I *did* need to date men who had a vocabulary that exceeded twenty words.

Of course, I'm sure *he* didn't figure that all these years later *I'd* do a lot of talking about that date from hell. But I am the Oracle. I want to leave this planet a better place. It's a public service. It's not just an act of diss and tell. I learned from my mistakes.

Now you can, too.

PART I

Dating

Your Coat of Armor

Before you even get to the dating part, you have to steel yourself. (Literally would help, but that metallic look is *so* 1981.) The first chapter can't be about what to do after your first date, because first we need to get you ready for that first date.

Think of yourself as Joan of Arc. She didn't prance around in the medieval equivalent of a slinky little Versace number and stilettos, but not because she wasn't a hot-looking chick. No, Joan knew she was living through very tough and dangerous times, so she always left the house with her coat of armor. You need to wake up and realize that these are very tough and dangerous times as well. Take it from Joan— let your guard down and you'll get burned.

What you need is your own coat of armor. When Joan went into battle, she grabbed her coat. When you go out on a date, you're doing the same thing. It's like you're going into minibattle. The last thing you want is to be underdressed and unprotected.

Men are tricky individuals. *They* are practically born with a coat of armor—they're thick headed and hard hearted. They're warriors, and most of them have no code of honor. (Say *honor* to them, and most will hear "on 'er.") So you need to have your own coat of armor, too—one that can't be penetrated until *you* want to be penetrated.

Your coat of armor consists of the valuable information you take with you in your brain cells, because knowledge is power and power is survival; a smart plan of attack, including an RFR (Rapid-Fire Response) system, so that no matter what the guy pulls on you, you'll be ready to react; and what you choose to put on your body plus all the other little physical preparations you make for a date. This first section will give you these pieces. I promise you—with a coat of armor this complete, you'll be immune to Cupid's harmful arrows.

Your coat of armor is like safe sex before the sex even happens.

Lesson 1

—————— • ——————

Know What Dating Is

DATING IS NEVER HAVING TO SAY "I'M LONELY"

I once was asked how I'd explain the concept of dating to space aliens. I guess the real answer is, "Is the alien single? Does he have a nice spaceship?"

I do think it's useful to start a book on dating by nailing down what exactly dating is in the first place. You've gotta know what you're up against before it's up against you.

Dating is one of two things. Either it's about trying to get to the next level or it's about trying to get laid. Dating and mating go hand in hand. You date, you mate. You mate, you keep the world procreating the way it's supposed to. Then, unless you stay with the same guy for eighty years and die in his arms—which is lovely, but if that's your plan you're reading the wrong book—the next logical step is extricating. All good—and most bad—things must come to an end.

Dating, mating, extricating, procreating . . . masturbating. . . . I'm a white rapper.

If dating is about trying to get to the next level, it makes sense that we take it so damn seriously. If we fail to get to the next level with a guy, it makes us feel like we're faulty, like we're broken people, like no man will ever have us. Dating is too important to take lightly. It's no walk in the park, though that can be a nice date if you're over sixty-five.

Dating is also a test of our ability to make a connection. It gives us a window into how men see us, and if they'd like to continue to see us on a regular basis.

And you were trying to pull it off without a manual? Good luck.

Wanna Get a Guy's Attention? Ignore Him!

HAPPY LANDINGS

My first date? I can't think back that far, to the Jurassic Era. I guess I probably arrived at the cave and the guy clubbed me, dragged me in by the hair, and had his way with me.

My first *real* date was my prom date with Bobby back in Hollywood, Florida, when my date showed up on a Harley and I was on quaaludes and in silver lamé and blue eye shadow. Times are different. Dates are not nearly so chill. You have to play the game if you want to win.

Let me give you a blow-by-blow of an experience I had with a hot pilot I met recently when I drove out to Malibu with a carful of my gay male buddies. It was supposed to be a day of walking along the beach (my favorite thing in life), looking for men (a close second), and just plain old relaxing. I didn't even want coffee—I'm forever trying to kick caffeine, but my posse needed a fix. That's when this drop-dead gorgeous pilot cruised by on the wooden deck of the little café we'd randomly chosen.

Bam! Those perfect pecs.

Bam! That strong jaw!

Bam! The sky-blue eyes . . . ink-black curly hair . . . worn leather bomber jacket resting on a firm, cute ass.

I had to remind myself to blink.

My sponsor was dangling on the other end of my cell phone (don't worry, caffeine is allowed). "I gotta go," I whispered. At that moment, I was confident that booze wasn't my problem anymore, which was a major win. But men? They were my addiction and the biggest threat to my sanity. The craving we all share for men will never change, but would we want it any other way? Oh, no. We just want to control that force of nature and make it work for us.

I managed to look away from him before he noticed my interest. He appreciated it when I completely ignored him—I was definitely on this pilot's radar. That's how you do it. Never invite a guy's attention. You must ignore him at first, so he wants to come to the party. A few minutes later, he moved his chair closer—while ignoring me back with a fake cell phone call.

It's the old dating dance.

Men have always known the power of ignoring women. You know all those guys you're dying to date who seem "so perfect and he doesn't even know it"? He knows it. And now you know it.

Forty-five tension-filled moments later, he was asking me out. It was a war of the wills—plus, he had to fight his way through this gay moat I had surrounding me. (My posse really makes guys work to approach the inner circle.) But I'd ignored him more completely than he'd ignored me. I won.

It didn't turn into true love; I didn't even marry the guy. But not every relationship is "the one." Some connections are just pleasant layovers for the evening, or the afternoon, and that's good enough. We had a pretty nice date on the beach the following weekend and kissed a few times in a sand dune. He didn't have a Harley, and I wasn't spinning in my prom dress, but it all worked out just the way I wanted—because I worked it.

If nothing else, think of it as practice. (And I've had a lot of practice.)

Lesson: Before you start thinking about another date, practice ignoring a man you're interested in. It's the ultimate aphrodisiac.

IGNORE AND CONQUER

For all of you who insist that there aren't any eligible, devastatingly gorgeous, remotely available men in the continental United States, the Oracle has this comment: You may be right.

Desperate times call for desperate measures. Wherever possible, they call for you to get out your passport and travel the globe to meet your dating destiny, which is what I did on a recent trip to Cape Town, South Africa.

From the start, the entire idea of going to wildlife-infested, seventeen-shots-before-you-go-there, ten-million-hour-plane-ride Africa (sorry, Bob Geldof) left me questioning my sanity. But this was a trip for *America's Next Top Model*, and when Miss Tyra Banks says you're going to Cape Town, you ask how high. Then you get out the Louis Vuitton luggage and someone starts packing for you.

Arriving late at night to shoot a few episodes, I was bleary-eyed and exhausted, but too tired to sleep. I was like Bill Murray in *Lost in Translation*, wandering in a foreign land—which is another way of saying I ditched the solitude of my hotel room to roam the lobby and all-night bar.

I met him on my first night. The pertinent details: Greek, chiseled jaw line, built, dark, brooding, twenty-two years old, shoulders like Hercules. But all of that was overwhelmed by the fact that he was living permanently in South Africa. My rational brain screamed, "There are long-distance relationships, and then there are impossibly long-distance relationships and just how many miles do I have in my United account for just plain relations?"

But I got over my rational brain and focused on this man, who looked like Michelangelo's David. He was working the hotel bar that night—and I mean *working* it: standing there shirtless, in sandals, shake-shake-shaking a martini. No shirt, no shoes, no problem.

Michelangelo, as I'll call him, was Colin Farrell from *Alexander* mixed with a little Brad Pitt from *Troy* with a few grape leaves in all the right places.

I had died and gone to Mount Olympus.

Here's how you do it when you want someone to be smitten with you in mere moments: You look, you smile, you sit in a pose that doesn't seem to be a pose, but any model knows you're posing. You move your chiffon dress a little bit north while you sit on the barstool, flashing some high-class thigh while rejoicing that you aren't prowling the hotel at all hours in jeans. Having planned ahead, you're wearing lilac, which is the color of spring—a fact lost on straight men, but one that inspires confidence in the woman wearing it.

This is how you continue to work it when he smiles back at you: You take your index finger and move it slightly, which is the universal signal for "come here."

He was shaking another drink as I did that, so he didn't move, but instead took his manly index finger and pointed it at me and tossed back the universal rejoinder: "No, *you* come *here*." He did this with a curling, full lip, which practically made me slide off my barstool.

This was no time to ignore my own rules, so I mouthed the words "No way, baby." And then I pointed back at him, giving him another invite to get his cute ass in gear and bridge the distance between the two of us. Then I upped the ante, turning to chat with two male crew members from *America's Next Top Model*, who were amused to be watching the Oracle in action.

After the initial contact, I dove into Ignore mode like a nuclear sub sinking into the Atlantic.

I wasn't wearing a watch, so I couldn't literally time the Greek's response. But in an estimated two New York seconds (that's ten in Greek seconds), he was at my side. Now that he was close, it really hit me: This man was so handsome there was a sex aura radiating from him. An orchestra seemed to be playing with each of his moves, a chorus of harps. I made a mental note to roll my own tongue back into my head. It's not cool not to play it cool.

"What's your name?" I asked him, as if I couldn't care less.

"Tiger," he replied (you can't make this shit up), leaning on the bar and invading my personal space—which I had no problem with.

"I'm Panther," I teased. Tacky is the new smooth.

"Would you like a drink?" he asked.

"I don't drink," I replied, crossing my legs. I speak body language, and crossing your legs says, "Never gonna get it," which makes a guy want it all the more. His eyes widened a bit, so I gave him a few more details. "No booze for me. No drugs. Love is my drug, baby."

After another six minutes of eye flirtations, it was clear that he wanted me and I wanted him. Here's how it went: I slid provocatively off the barstool like I was packing it up for the night and those eye caresses were all he was getting for the evening, or maybe even forever. Clearly, Tiger was feeling caged; he couldn't even pretend to be cool by ignoring our chemistry.

"You're leaving?" he practically shouted. Then he did something so damn sexy that it stopped me in my tracks: He jutted out his bottom lip in a little-boy pout. Clearly, this was his standard move, one that had worked many times before, but I have to give him an A-plus anyway: That boy was very, very good at the art of the pout.

But I just turned away and walked directly out the door.

Here's the thing: In that position, you *must* leave. You must play out the game. You can't just jump from first base to home plate. You need to hit all the bases in between if it's ever going to get good.

Before the door slammed, I caught it, turned back, and waved, without really looking at him. He was still pouting—I could feel that bottom lip even though my back was turned. I took the elevator—alone—up to my room.

Suddenly, South Africa was one of my favorite places on earth.

Tyra had promised us the primal beauty of native wildlife, but I don't think this was necessarily what she had in mind.

The next night, I returned to the bar in a sultry black dress with an uninterested look on my face and a huge hunk of man by my side. Tiger didn't have any way of knowing it, but my escort wasn't my date: He was my bodyguard, six foot five and built like a brick shithouse.

Tiger was shaking his martini shaker, and his ass, when we strolled in. When he got a load of us, he went beyond pouting and straight to pissed.

Sitting on a barstool, I loudly put him out of his misery. "Duke, you can go now. I'll be fine. I don't think I'll need any guarding for the next few minutes," I said.

Tiger went from depressed to impressed in twenty words or less.

"You're that international supermodel," he said, putting down a mineral water with a wedge of lime in front of me. I didn't even have to order it.

"We're here to film a TV show and they've given me a body-guard . . . and an international cell phone," I said, getting out a pen and writing my new number on a piece of paper.

Game over.

For six days, we had a mad, passionate affair. He made love to me 24/7. Everyone on the show kept asking about him. Let me put it to you this way: He was a guy, but he could have been *America's Next Top Model* if he wanted to be—he had my vote.

How was he in bed? He ruled the 1,000-count sheets. And speaking of numbers . . . I told him I was thirty-two.

Either he believed it or he didn't even care. We were both too busy counting orgasms.

The point is, if I hadn't acted bored with him at first, he might never have been interested in the first place. I gave him a challenge—myself—and he took it.

Lesson 3

Broadcast It

PUTTING IT OUT THERE

If I could, would I live and love on an island with all women? We could spend the days working out, discussing beauty tips, and taking long baths each night in that little cove with the natural hot spring. I'm sure Paradise Island would be lovely for a time, but you'd *have* to be a Wonder Woman not to miss men, those bastards who despite all their crap are basically all potential boyfriends.

But how do you get a man to take an active interest in you—beyond noticing you ignoring him from across the room?

I get asked out everywhere, anywhere, all day long. I get hit on a *number* of times a day—airplanes, taxis, the deli, nightclubs. I mean, it's crazy. What can I say? There's no chronological shelf-life for a supermodel.

Some men are model collectors. They act like they don't know I'm a model, just so they can do the whole "I fell in love with *you*, not who you are" routine. Then they take me home with them and I find they've got a shrine of my old *Cosmo* covers in their bedroom.

But men don't ask me out just because of my career. Let's face it, how many men who want to get with me know anything about my work with Francesco Scavullo? The ones who have no clue that I'm a supermodel want to hook up with the Big Dog because I give them a vibe that says, "I'm a fun date."

You have to broadcast to men that you're ready, willing, and (avail)able.

Once you've mastered the ignoring part and gotten his attention, you have to telegraph your interest. Let him know you're interested, giving him steady eye contact and directing the conversation. Don't bat your eyes and act all, "Oh, you're so smart!" with him—fuck that! Take the lead and the guy will be all over you.

Sure, some guys like idiots who coo at everything they say. A lot of guys love that type. But you want nothing to do with that type. Don't fake it just to get a man's interest—stealth dating will just get you involved with a jerk.

Here's an example: The story of how I once let a guy know I was in the mood for dude, in well under a minute . . . and all from the safety of my car!

I was driving my Mercedes SUV down Mulholland on an overcast Saturday morning before Christmas when I noticed a 911 moment if there ever was one. There he was, a six-two firefighter with sandy blond hair and what I call x-ray pecs—pecs so big and hard and defined you feel like you can see every inch of them right through the skintight shirt that's struggling to contain them. That's right, I'm a boob girl.

This red-hot fireman was right there by the side of the road. I have to say, the fireman fantasy that all women have (and many men embrace, too) ain't a myth. Firemen aren't just hot because they happen to look like beefy *GQ* models. They're also the bravest men in the world, which just makes them the best of the best on the male food chain. They can heat you up like no other, and you know they have the strength to lift you in their strong arms and carry you to bed to douse whatever four-alarm fires they find there.

BRB—I need to go get some cold water.

Okay. Back to the side of the road. I was in flirting overdrive that morning, thanks to the full moon the night before, so there was never any question that I'd swing my SUV to the side of the road and pull right up to the shiny red fire engine bumper. I rolled down my window and feigned a look of serious concern. (All without furrowing my brows too much—I don't need some casual flirtation giving me wrinkles.)

The closer inspection paid off: He had a square jaw; big, pillowy lips; and huge, blue eyes. He didn't see me giving him the once-over because he was too busy handling his hose—by which I mean the giant yellow contraption he was using to pour city water out onto someone's lawn. I thought about lending a hand.

I felt the smoke rise in myself, although there didn't appear to be any flames in the vicinity unless you counted the ones shooting from my eyes.

I wondered if he'd been trained to withstand the intensity of the heat I was feeling. But I couldn't wonder too long, because there are times when you have to make a move. Remember, men aren't mind-readers, even when we're sending our best signals their way. You'd have to hold up a sign saying, "Come on over here and grab me!" for some of them to get the picture.

"Excuse me," I said in the sweetest voice you've ever heard. My fireman glanced in the direction of my SUV and sparks flew. He dropped his hose and moved closer. I just love it when city workers remember that we taxpayers come first.

"What's happening here? Is something on fire?" I asked my fireman. It's a miracle I was able to speak, with that face of his inches from mine. I was in the driver's seat of my car—and of the situation, I guess, because all of a sudden he seemed very concerned with his civic duty. "Can I help?" he asked.

It was highly unlikely I'd be getting out of my SUV to help—I don't think I could run up a ladder in my daytime Manolo pumps.

"Miss, everything is fine, but it's very kind of you to be so concerned," he said, smiling like he was posing for the annual fireman's beefcake calendar. *Faux* relief flooded my face, as if I'd been worried that Los Angeles was about to burn to a crisp. The truth is, the only thing smoldering was the look I was giving him now that I'd ditched my Gucci sunglasses.

"We're just practicing here so we can be ready in case some day a beautiful woman like you needs some saving," said my fireman. His behavior could be summed up in three words: flirt, flirt, flirt.

I didn't skip a beat. I didn't take a breath. He put it out there, and I had no choice but to volley it right back at him—RFR, baby, Rapid-Fire Response.

"Are you really sure there isn't *anything* I can do to help you out?" I asked, a tad suggestively. I wasn't afraid to give as good as I was getting. Two volleys and it was time to make a move—banter spoils faster than milk in the sun.

He smiled. I winked. Time to take it to a higher level.

"Maybe you could help me . . . have a beer later," he suggested.

"Maybe some coffee," I replied, with a mental nod to my sponsor. It's okay to throw a guy a curveball in these situations—you don't have to agree to whatever he suggests. Show him a little bit of your own ego, and before you know it you'll be comparing ids.

He scribbled his number down on his fireman's pad that he used to write reports for emergencies. Nice touch. Now I felt like an official emergency.

I smiled again, took the number, and drove off. He was a fireman, so I figured he'd be familiar with this move—light him up, peel off, stir up the embers for later. I checked my watch: only 10:00 A.M., and my flirting mojo was already in overdrive. I had the whole day left to continue collecting phone numbers. It was time to move on.

Girls, if you don't call 911, how is a guy gonna know you're on fire?

Put Yourself First

BUT ENOUGH ABOUT YOU

Remember, you are your own first dating priority. It's not about them. It's about you, you, you.

My best friend, Jon Lovitz, jokes, "We have a short time on this planet, Janice, which is why I ask, 'What about me?' "

Women make the mistake of always thinking it's about the man. When it's too much about the man, it's time to call for the check.

It's okay to be a little selfish. It's also fine to be a woman at the half-century mark, like myself, and set the Valentino tablecloth with one place setting. I'm fine with that, because I'm happy with myself. If someone comes along who's happy with me as I am, then you're dating the real me. We'll all be happy and no one will have to call for the check.

Now let's try to figure out where to meet a man who deserves half of your Valentino tablecloth.

———◆———

How to Find a Guy (or The One to Read If You're Flipping Through This Book in the Store)

GOING ON A MANHUNT

Before we get too deep into the how-tos of actual dating, you've got to start with a man. Even God had to start with a man—the one He made perfect (allegedly) in His image. So the same goes for you.

Next question: Where to meet one? Girls come up to me all the time asking me where they can meet men. My response is, "Are you off your rocker? No? Then get off your rocker and you might meet a few men for a change."

You can meet men *anywhere*. But if you want to meet *good* men, follow my advice and pick and choose which places you go when you're in full search-and-enjoy mode.

Top Three Requirements for a Perfect Man

- SLIM HIPS
- FLEXIBLE SCHEDULE
- TRUST FUND

Not necessarily in that order.

TOP TEN PLACES TO MEET (GOOD) MEN

(10) PARK BENCHES. No, I'm not that desperate—I'm not talking about bums (well, except that all men are . . . oh, skip it). But a park bench is a perfectly good place to meet the man of your dreams. Cute guys hang out in the park. The rich ones *own* parks. Find one to flirt with, and then when you're done you can work off your frustration with a nice run.

(9) MEN'S CLOTHING STORES. I'm not talking about Today's Man. Go to Turnbull & Asser, where they make beautiful handmade shirts for men. They've dressed everyone from the Prince of Wales to James Bond, believe it or not. You won't find any slouches there. You'll find metrosexuals with big bank accounts and no hangups about spending cash on quality merchandise—that's where I come in.

(8) BIKE PATHS. I love to go bike riding. Like having sex, riding a bike is something you never forget how to do once you learn. Men like to see a woman who's active—and it's a good excuse to show off your legs.

(7) THE CAR WASH. Don't laugh! A car wash is like a fucking sea of love, and it's a great place to see and be seen. It's perfect for a germophobe like me. The most fabulous car wash I know is one in Boys Town, a.k.a. West Hollywood, near my house in California. The car wash guys are so beautiful I give them twenty bucks just to say my name. Of course, most of my car wash guys are gay, but that's just my neighborhood. At most car washes, you should have no problem finding a few straight guys to say your name for free.

(6) DOG PARKS. Dog parks are practical places to meet men. At least you know the men can handle the responsibility of nurturing and interacting with living things. (You also know they're used to dealing with some crap.) It's okay to visit a dog park even if you don't own a dog. If someone asks, tell 'em yours is in the shop. (No one ever questions my being there, pooch or no pooch; everyone knows Janice *is* the Big Dog.)

All this dog talk reminds me of how guys are always comparing themselves to dogs, acting like they *have* to have sex, as if that's some kind of an excuse for any disgusting behavior or disloyal shenanigans. You just tell them, if they have to walk the dog, you have to walk the kitty, too, girls. In fact, Kitty may even need to go out on a rhinestone leash. . . .

(5) THE GYM. The gym can be a terrific place to meet men. Men who work out are likely to be excellent time managers, have less stress in their lives, and oh, yeah—they're often the proud owners of biceps that can crack walnuts. I enjoy lounging at the Equinox Gym in West Hollywood, in a 5,000-thread-count white towel, looking very Elizabeth Taylor circa Mike Todd.

The purpose of such lounging, of course, is to pick up well-toned men. But even the Oracle has to remember that real estate isn't the only field where it's all about location, location, location. Yes, you're surrounded by gorgeous, fit, tanned men at the gym, but so are they—and some of them might like that as much as you do. This is a very common problem, which is why the gym ranks only number 5 on my list, even though the good guys you *do* meet usually make up for all the false alarms.

How do I get my gaydar in gear? If they're checking *each other* out and not withering in the presence of my Liz-ness, I'm aware of it. If a man asks you about your moisturizer, chances are he's not a good prospect. The straight men around aren't thinking about their own skin; they're thinking about mine, reclining on the seafoam green couch looking all perky and glistening from the sauna.

The moral of the story: Be careful even when you're going to a seemingly Janice-approved venue for meeting men. Gay male friends can be the bomb, but don't you have enough friends already? You don't need my help finding new shopping buddies.

(4) THE BANK. It can't be just any old bank—it has to be a main branch of one of the most exclusive banks out there, as approved by *Forbes*. Track one down immediately, and make yourself more of a fixture in the lobby than a potted palm. Find out where Sumner Redstone or Warren Buffett or Rupert Murdoch have their checking accounts, and check it out yourself. Sure, they're probably taken, but their wealthy friends and all their little aspiring-CEO fans might bank there, too. You have to have a lot of cash to be banking there, and the ones who do might be looking for someone to spend a little time with—or a little money on. Just make sure they understand there's a substantial penalty for early withdrawal.

(3) DELICATESSENS IN WEALTHY NEIGHBORHOODS. Madonna's business partner, Guy Oseary, once wrote a book called *Jews Who Rock*. I didn't get it—to me, all Jewish men rock!

For Janice, it's all about the Jews. They respect quality, they have great senses of humor, they know about humility, and what else? Oh, yeah—they're hung longer than the Bible. I call them my *oy* toys.

(2) THE GOLF COURSE ON WEEKDAYS. Only two types of men can golf on weekdays: rich men and retired men, who are often rich men too. The rich can skip work on a daily basis and golf. Doctors generally consider golf a mandatory part of their jobs. Rich guys have obvious charms. Even putting the financial picture aside, retired guys are a plus because they can devote themselves to you 24/7. Wanna get a guy to shoot for a hole in one? Wear your cutest, frilliest skirt and bend over to pick up the ball while putting. Ask guys if you can borrow their ball washer. Just showing up and looking good will put you in the green and within putting distance of a man.

(1) CAR DEALERSHIPS. Mercedes dealerships, BMW dealerships, jet dealerships—basically, anywhere there's a dealership, there's a man. Hang out by the parts department looking really good and men will flock to you, eager to trade their parts for yours. Men in dealerships have money. Guys don't go car shopping unless they have the bread to back it up; otherwise, it just makes them feel depressed and inadequate. Do men see cars as reflections of their packages? Absolutely.

On that note . . . maybe you can find yourself a limo dealership.

From my own experience, I can vouch for car dealerships. My Mercedes truck has become a total lemon; I really should trade it in. But I don't want to get rid of it, and not because it's a status symbol in Los Angeles. The truth is, that damn SUV is a man magnet—a steel-clad guarantee that I'll meet my weekly quota of choice members of the opposite sex.

And here's the thing: Now that the fucking thing breaks down every other minute, I'm constantly sitting in my Mercedes dealership, sipping lattes and meeting fascinating men who drive cars even hotter than mine.

Of course, I can't be sure these men are rich. I don't know if they're good men, either. But at least I know they're men with good taste. And just sitting in that service center is better than surfing the Web for weeks. Just imagine if the dealerships could advertise the full extent of their services: "We'll rotate your tires and work on giving you a future lube job!"

A Closer Look: Are Jewish Men God's Gift?

The answer is oy, give me those Jewish boys! They make the absolute *best* husbands—because they're loyal and because they have the largest units. What more do you want?

Jewish men clearly didn't go white in a certain area, which makes them fabulous mates. But they're also good in the long run, because Jewish men are used to women running things. You can take control and you'll never hear them gripe, because their grandmothers did it to their grandfathers, their mothers did it to their fathers, their sisters did it to their brothers-in-law. You get the idea.

Jewish men are also used to the woman taking charge of the household finances, so you'll control the purse strings—which are always strings I want to control. They're also less likely to divorce you. They would rather put up with more of your crap than give you the keys to the second BMW and the vacation house in Boca.

Of course, there *is* all that Jewish guilt. Of course, that in itself is no reason to call for the check; after all, Jewish men have no monopoly on guilt. Catholic men, Muslim men, Mormons—they're all fucking guilty. It's the same no matter what religion or culture we're dissecting. All men have a certain amount of guilt, and it has nothing to do with religion. Would you rather be with a man who's guilty with nothing in his Calvins, or a man who's guilty with a huge package? I'd take the latter. And have.

Now let's focus on a topic most Jewish men will bring up eventually with shiksa girlfriends who are potential wife material. He'll probably want you to convert. Does this mean no more Christmas trees, no more curling up on Santa's lap? Depends. Some Jewish men can deal with a tree, as long as their mother is several states away or dead. They'll even let you put up a few lights around the house, as long as you say it's for "the holidays."

On the plus side, Christmas is only one day; there are seven nights to Hanukkah. When it comes to gifts, you do the math.

(continued)

Of course, when I got engaged to my Jewish soon-to-be husband Simon, I lied and told him I would convert. Deep down, I knew it probably wasn't in me: I might exchange my BMW for a Range Rover, my Dolce for Chanel. But when it came converting to another religion, I was feeling a little *verklempt*.

I did pretend to convert for a little while, but deep down my heart was singing "White Christmas." Simon seemed a smidge annoyed when I refused to gag down gefilte fish, but I lied and told him it just had too many grams of fat. Potato latkes? Did he want me fitting into his family or my jeans? He chose the jeans.

I think there ought to be a reality show about Christian women converting to Judaism. Of course, there isn't a network that would touch it. But it might be interesting to watch some skinny WASP woman in Connecticut trying to make a brisket heavier than she is.

Personally, I don't think a religious difference is a good enough reason to call for the check. One of my best girlfriends is Catholic, but she celebrates Hanukkah. If you're in a family unit, you do things for the sake of the children. And who knows? You might actually enjoy it.

Top Ten Worst Places to Meet Guys

(10) FAMILY REUNIONS. This is kinda self-explanatory. And yes, cousins count.

(9) AA. Men are an addiction in and of themselves. If you're at an AA meeting, honey, it's time to *focus!*

(8) FUNERALS. If I said you had a beautiful body, would you hold it against me? (Sorry, that was gross—even for me.)

(7) OUTLET MALLS. A little low rent for my taste.

(6) TRAFFIC LIGHTS. Guys just aren't themselves behind the wheel of a car. They have a bullshit *American Graffiti* fantasy that makes them all think they're Mario Andretti. Get them on a date and you'll be flashing them a stale yellow within five minutes.

(5) WORK. Don't shit where you eat—simple as that. (And, no, I don't care how degrading that metaphor is to the act of love between a man and a woman.)

(4) FAST-FOOD DRIVE-THROUGH WINDOWS. Because if you keep eating fast food, good luck finding a guy.

(3) JAIL. Prison is never a good place to find yourself, let alone a man.

(2) THE INTERNET. You know how they used to say of ugly actors, "He has a face for radio?" Well, if a guy's out there hunting for women online, chances are he has a face and personality for the Web. Plus, some of those weirdos really could be *hunting* for women. And remember this: If the camera adds ten pounds, the Web adds forty.

(1) BAKERIES. Unless you really wanna meet a fat slob whose idea of a hot night out is hanging out around the ovens where they make doughnuts and cupcakes and that thick bread they use to make French toast.

But Janice, you ask, *what am I supposed to do if I don't own a Mercedes?* You can still show up at the service place! Insist that you're waiting to give your rich brother or business partner a lift home after he drops off his car. That'll give you plenty of chatting time while you wait. When he doesn't show, you can simply say, "I guess he got a limo to pick him up."

These are some of my best stack-the-deck places to meet mates, but the truth is that you can meet a guy anywhere, anytime. For that reason, you should make sure you have mascara and lip gloss on at all times—even that "no makeup" look is always enhanced by these two simple ingredients.

The strangest place I ever met a guy was on a long, long escalator. He was going up and I was going down. (Funny, I often advise women to go down when they find a man who's on his way up.) He was staring at my legs, which is how I knew I had him cold. He pointed at his ring finger, which was not only empty but had no tan line to suggest that he'd hastily tugged off and hidden a wedding band. I pointed at mine, which was also ring free. Then, just as we were about to pass each other on those moving stairs, he gave me the perfect pitch—literally: He flicked me his business card, which landed on my outstretched palm.

You gotta love destiny.

I called him three days later. Why the wait? I had a lot of shopping to do!

Lesson 6

The Pickup

LINE, PLEASE!

Men are like actors—they feel they're nothing without good lines. They will say literally anything to get your attention.

Forget about men and their lines. Once it's obvious the sparks are flying, I always recommend making the first move. I ask men out all the time. I met my last boyfriend, Tommy, on the set of *The Surreal Life*. I was asked to do that show because I'm ratings gold. (What kind of ratings? Somewhere between NC-17 and X, when I can get away with it.) I agreed to do it for the cash. But the unexpected bonus was Tommy. We had to ignore each other for twelve days, because his contract forbade him to speak with the cast. I'm a rule breaker by nature, but not when it comes to signed contracts. So we followed the rules.

But the minute he was off the show, I hit him with one of my favorite pickup lines. I said, "Dude, are you straight or gay?" He replied, "I'm *straight*." So I asked him for coffee and we arranged to go out. Some bitches keep the clothes after they do a show—I keep a member of the crew.

You have to initiate things in this life. If you see a guy you like, you have to take the lead—because guys are basically stupid, as some of *their* choice pickup lines prove.

Top Ten Shitty Pickup Lines . . . And How to Put Them Down

(10) "I MUST BE IN HEAVEN . . . BECAUSE YOU'RE AN ANGEL." For some reason, this line works on lots of women. Something about being called an "angel" turns girls into suckers. Literally. But this line's sheer cliché factor should turn you off. You're reading it in a book, babe, and he probably did, too. Which means he's not looking for an angel, he's looking to get laid. Tell him, "You're not in heaven, and that's not the direction you're heading, either."

---

(9) "WHAT DO YOU DO FOR A LIVING . . . BESIDES LOOK-ING SEXY?" This one is easy for me, because that *is* what I do for a living. But if you're not a supermodel, come back with, "I moonlight with the bull-shit police and you're under arrest."

---

(8) "IS THAT YOUR CAR PARKED OUTSIDE?" When a guy truly has nothing to say and no imagination, something generic like this is his call-ing card. Just reply smoothly, "No, it's my boyfriend's. Why? Is it giving you a complex?"

---

(7) "I DON'T NEED PICKUP LINES, BABY. I JUST SMILE AND PLAY DUMB." This is usually a reply to a bad reaction to their first pickup line. If they use this, that makes them zero for two. I don't believe in giving three strikes when it comes to pickup lines—two is more than fair. You say, "I don't need pickup lines, either. I just smile and walk away."

---

(6) "I JUST INHERITED $500 MILLION AND I NEED SOME-ONE TO SPEND IT ON." This one is hard to resist, even if you're not a born gold digger. But how likely is it that a guy who just inherited half a bil-

lion bucks is hanging out in a polo shirt and a gold chain with no idea how to manscape his bushy eyebrows? Tell him, "Why don't you spend it on yourself? I know a great plastic surgeon."

(5) "YOU MAKE ME WANT TO BE A BETTER MAN. LET'S START NOW." For all of you who love changing guys, this line was invented for you. Resist it with, "I can't—I'm too busy being a better woman than that."

(4) "MY WIFE JUST LEFT ME." Sad and pathetic and just very common. It reminds me of my second marriage! Tell him, "She had a point."

(3) "I LOOK SO GOOD I DON'T NEED A PICKUP LINE." Especially offensive if the guy is a toad on top of being an egomaniac, but even a good-looking guy has no business being so up front with you. Say, "I don't like stand-up comedy."

(2) "NICE LEGS. WHAT TIME DO THEY OPEN?" Just gross. "Try our new location on No Fucking Way."

(1) "YOUR FEET MUST BE TIRED BECAUSE YOU WERE RUNNIN' THROUGH MY DREAMS LAST NIGHT." This is the all-time most overused BS pickup line. You've got every right to say, "Oh, are we making up country song titles? How about: 'All I Want From You Is Away.'"

Positive Pickup RFR

If the right guy asks for your number, don't say, "Yeah, sure." What's that mean, anyway? You: "Mandatory." I'm like a Magic 8 Ball sometimes:

"Mandatory." "Of course." "Ask me later." "It appears not to be known." "Mandatory" works as a reply to almost anything anyone could ever ask. Extreme? Maybe. But I'm not a halfway kind of girl.

Negative Pickup RFR

HOW TO KILL HIS INTEREST

We've all had guys we really want nothing to do with try hitting on us. The best way to put them off? Tell them you have a boyfriend. Seems simple, but it's an instant, all-purpose turnoff. And if it's not, he's even worse than you think. Just shut down and go into Deep Ignore mode. If *that* fails, tell him he makes you want to throw up.

If you're really hurting for something to say, don't overthink it. One of my favorite icebreakers is simple and suggestive without being phony: "What's shakin'?"

PULL THE CAREER LADDER OUT FROM UNDER HIM

I was at the Coffee Bean & Tea Leaf in Los Angeles and this John-John-type hunk in a blue tailored suit, red tie, and striped shirt sauntered by the world's first supermodel. He didn't look at me, which made me steam like a cappuccino maker.

Obviously, he was the kind of guy who felt he was so hot he didn't need to waste precious eye movement—who felt he should be the object of stares, not the starer.

I've seen this peacock type many times before; haven't we all? These men have a way of revealing themselves, but *you* need to watch for the clues.

First: As soon as your brain registers that he's gorgeous, it's time for Ignore mode. When we see something beautiful, we tend to look at it; our pupils widen. When you get that little burst of excitement that tells you a hot guy is in your field of vision, train yourself to react as if the total opposite is happening. Do not look interested. Do not look, period.

Peacock was sneaking glances at me, which I could tell out of the corner of my eye, but he was pretending not to notice me as he picked up his latte and took a seat way in the back of the coffee place. He was about ten years younger than I was, which as the French say is *pas important* (translation: Who the fuck cares?). But hang on. Within a few minutes, some witch with long blonde hair in a yoga outfit had spied my hot man and started shaking her ass in his direction. He was fake-ignoring me, but he was real-ignoring her. Honey, throwing yourself at a peacock is never the right approach.

If Peacock were a regular man, I could have walked over and said, "Nice shirt. Where did you get it? I'd love to get one for my brother." That would be like saying, "Hi, I think you're hot, and the only man in my life shares my DNA." But he's a peacock and they're excitable, so you have to lure them in slowly.

When you feel the urge to approach a peacock, remind yourself, "I should be the center of the universe, not him." That's what I was thinking—*hard*—as I ignored the noise of my hormones barking like unfed puppies. I was so focused on not focusing on him that I accidentally picked up some disgusting tea concoction for a girl named Allison.

"Who is Allison?" I called out across the place. Peacock seemed amused. I'd done something that forced him to notice me, but I hadn't spoken to him directly. He was staring at me. Maybe with admiration.

Allison identified herself, but she didn't want the tea now that someone had scooped it up by mistake. (What did she think, I contaminated it? Fuck you very much, Allison.) "Honey, I don't have a disease," I told her, trading for my own skim milk latte. She backed down and took her secondhand tea. Peacock watched the entire exchange openly, but then things got interesting: He went to the men's room. People say I'm ballsy, but I couldn't follow him in there.

It was time for an advanced move. This move takes guts. It's for risk-takers. Once you pull this move, you can't hesitate.

I left the Coffee Bean, like I didn't care if I ever saw him again.

I didn't go very far—I knew I had to be outside when he got out of the john. The effect of my sudden absence should be enough, I thought, to put him over the edge and reel him in.

I was out by a parking meter on my cell phone, telling a girlfriend about my adventures in peacock hunting, when Peacock himself blessed the world with his presence. He walked outside and looked hard at me as I stood by my car, chatting away without a care in the world.

Just to really ruffle Peacock's feathers, I said loudly, "Tell them no—I don't want that film. I want an *action* film." He shyly came closer. I amped it up. "No, that one's too raunchy for me. I've already got that sex tape they keep threatening to put out." I started wrapping up the conversation, waiting for him to make his move already as I tacked on a final flourish: "Yeah, I know he was Madonna's ex. What am I supposed to do about that?"

By now Peacock was hovering near me, but still he seemed unable to speak. Finally, he came right up to me and looked me in the eye. He didn't say the first words, but it was as close to a first move as I was ever gonna get.

"Where did you get your stripes?" I asked, pointing to his striped shirt.

"Ted Baker in London," he replied smoothly.

"So you travel?" I said, mentally figuring out how we could go to Paris together on our first date.

"I was on a job," he replied in a way that begged me to keep digging.

"So you're a pilot?" I suggested hopefully, thinking my kids and I could all travel free. I never even saw it coming.

"I'm a model," he said proudly.

Can't I ever get away from my own type? All this and he was a dime-a-dozen male model?

"That's coincidental," I said dryly. "Me too."

"Well, I'm not *really* a model . . . yet," he said, smiling finally. Wow, he finally gave up some teeth. "I'd like to be a model. I'm hoping to sign with the Ford Agency." Aha. He was the only thing worse than a male model: an aspiring male model. And even though he obviously knew who I was, he didn't know enough about me to know that "Ford Agency" and "Janice Dickinson" don't belong in the same sentence anymore.

At that moment, figuring the career chit-chat was played out, he was acting like a regular guy again—and staring right into my tits.

"Would you like to go out sometime?" he asked them.

"I don't think so," I replied. My gut said no, and my tits weren't thrilled either. In case I was unfairly punishing him for trying to make me the first rung on his ladder of success, I accepted his number. He had clearly expected a much warmer reception. Peacock had spread his feathers, but I wasn't spreading back. He wanted to be a model, but he was really just a poser.

If a guy's first topic of conversation with you is career related, fuck that. You're not a career counselor. Check, please!

Lesson 7

Getting Ready for Your Date

PREDATE RITUALS

Once you get a date, don't blow it by showing up without giving the thing some thought. (You're reading a whole book on the subject—a step in the right direction.)

If you're going to bother to go out on a date, you must be on point!

People ask me what to do to prepare for a date. Number one, *douche*. (Sorry, I'm not into grunge fucking.) Number two, make sure you're bush-whacked: mandatory shaved box. *Manda*. I wanted this book to come with a boxed pussy-/ball-shaving set, I'm so passionate about this topic. They didn't go for it.

But you might not even *get* to that on a date—on the average date, he's got a good four hours to deep-six his chances. So, just for a moment, let's get our minds out of the gutter and focus on something more important: You must psych yourself up!

You know how to do it. Some do it with a drink (just one, girls, and not if the drink isn't your friend); some do it with an eight-mile run; some do it with a yoga class. Hell, have a cigarette if it helps. I like to call up one of my favorite designers and have him send me a hot new dress he has lying around. If you don't have their number, hitting Gucci or your favorite store is a little more expensive, but it works just as well at giving you that needed burst of energy. Do whatever you must, but get that adrenalin going—get that glint in your eye, that twinkle.

You need to get massages. I love massages. (Just drink a lot of water afterward.) I can see why guys want happy endings—a massage is an amazing way to unlock yourself before a big event, especially a date.

If all else fails, try some Gregorian chants: "nah-dah-dee-dah—*rich men*—nah-dah-dee-dah."

The point is that you should put some thought and effort into your date if you hope to encounter a guy who's put some thought and effort into you.

IF YOU DON'T LOOK GOOD . . . YOU DON'T LOOK GOOD

How do I prepare for a big date? Three hours of hair and makeup and careful, strategic wardrobe planning.

There's no such thing as casual dating—at least not until you've already done the walk of shame. If we're talking about a legit dating setup, then you have to treat each date like it's your last chance to find true love, babe. Make it count. Make an impression. Show up looking like you just rolled out of bed, and you'll be rolling back into it alone.

Groom for yourself, not for the guy. When you're spending $100 to get your hair blown out, don't think of it as a dating expense. (If only we could deduct this shit from our taxes.) Think of it as a kind of blow job you're getting for yourself. The same goes for getting your teeth professionally whitened or a fake tan sprayed on: You're doing it for *you*.

You're not living your life for men. You're living it for you. If a man comes along to enjoy your life, your body, your *you*—well, that's his dumb luck.

By the same token, when you work out, you should be working out for yourself. If I hear one more woman tell me she's in the gym seven days a week for her man, I'm going to take a ten-pound barbell and say, "Think fast!"

Are you *really* sweating for him? Are you contorting yourself through three days a week of yoga for a guy? If you are, that's pathetic. It's about *you*—your bod, your health, your mental well-being. If someone with a penis comes along to enjoy it, well, let him hit the gym the next day so he can look good for you.

Random notes: Shave your pits. Ladies, don't forget this step. You've probably run into a few men who've been put off by it—whether you know it or not—and you know what? I wouldn't want to sleep with you, either. And while you're at it, grab a Q-tip and get those blackheads out of your nose and ears.

READY TO WEAR

There's really no such thing as a good first-date uniform. We all have outfits we're most comfortable in, but you have to tailor what you wear

Janice D's Walk of Shame Survival Kit

If you know in advance there's gonna be a morning after, don't leave home without the following items, in a tiny bag, hidden on your person:

- TINY, ROLLED-UP SKIRT
- FRESH G-STRING
- HOT LITTLE FUCKIN' TANK
- TOOTHBRUSH AND TOOTHPASTE
- MAKEUP AND MAC MAKEUP REMOVER
- MOISTURIZER

(or get sewn into) depending on the dating situation. I've done formal dates and I've done casual, but even casual for me isn't casual. I'm not pulling on a Stones T-shirt and some jeans I haven't washed in a month and meeting some guy at Wendy's, you know. I'm engaging in a mutual seduction and I'm seeing how far it will go. That's a very different thing.

Once, I showed up on a date in a couture Karl Lagerfeld miniskirt and thigh-high boots and fishnets and bangled earrings, looking really hot, and the very conservative investment banker I was dating proceeded to tell me, "You're not wearing *that* to dinner." I was like, *"Pourquoi pas?"* He said, "Because you look like a hooker."

I looked expensive; he looked free. So who, I ask you, was more inappropriately dressed?

"Well, then maybe I should charge you," I said. How dare *he* talk to *me* about *my* wardrobe? "Maybe I shouldn't go out to dinner with *you* looking like *that*." Now he was sorry he'd opened his mouth.

When it comes to how men dress, it varies from guy to guy. My current boyfriend wears T-shirts and jeans; I don't like someone stodgy. But I do like tuxedoes on men. I think the wardrobe should be right for the environment, or the event, or the subtext of what's going on behind the green door.

The way you look always matters, and anyone who says it doesn't is a liar. It even matters what you look like in the bathroom. You have to have class with the way you look—even if you're standing there stark naked.

My son's hilarious on the subject of what goes on in the john. "No wife or girlfriend of mine will ever fart or shit in front of me!" he says, and it's actually a good rule. The minute you let your guard down in relationships or dating, or start to become slovenly with the way you eat—or the minute your guy forgets that he's supposed to be opening the door or holding a chair for you, chewing with his mouth open . . . well, those are dealbreakers.

Lesson 8

Stack the Odds

SEDUCING OR SEDUCED?

To illustrate how important seduction is to me, let me introduce you to my Italian Stallion (no, not *that* Italian Stallion—been there, done that). This Italian Stallion was a blond John Travolta, thirties, *sooo* not in the mob. He arranged to meet me for business purposes, but it was clear from the second I saw him that he wanted to mount the Big Dog.

We met with our entourages at a club, and he sat down next to me. It was a roomful of people, straight and gay alike—it was fabulous, like the old Studio 54 days. He sat down by me. I was in couture like a tranny, with big hair, lashes, and nails, everything—perfect.

When he sat next to me, before anything else I felt this *energy*. Have you ever experienced this? It's that energy that makes people tick, the contentment that I crave, desire, and have been searching for my whole life. It was like every hair follicle stood on end, like every pore was opening—especially the Big Pore.

I looked him over as introductions were made: This was one well-groomed, blond, blue-eyed, chiseled Stallion. I was thinking, *I'm gonna have that for breakfast, eat some more for lunch, slug the rest down with some Jack Daniel's!* His pecs were bulging out of his Armani jacket. His

Seduction First-Aid Kit

I don't care if you're on date number one or date number one thousand, you must focus on the seduction. It doesn't have to be a three-ring circus, and it doesn't have to lead to sex (wait, do blow jobs count or not? I can't tell anymore), but whatever your speed, you have to incorporate some kind of seduction into your dating life. I've used every type of seduction in the book. That said, I'm here to say that the basics still work, which is why they've been around for so long.

- CANDLES ANYWHERE AND EVERYWHERE
- WINE (UNLESS YOU DON'T DRINK)
- SCENTED BATH PRE-DATE

face—well, it should have been on a stamp, that's how good it was. It ought to be on a poster so every young girl in America can have it on her wall and look up and think, "I want that."

Well, this walking stamp spoke to me, and whatever he said, it was like he was really saying, "Hi, I'm a straight boy and I'm gonna take care of you." (Not that gay guys wouldn't take care of you—they're actually better keepers. But I mean *take care of* you.) He was saying something about meeting me for a business deal, but that wasn't *really* what he was saying. It was a fraud, a way to get to meet me. He was seducing me.

The Stallion proceeded to watch me. Everyone in the club was coming up to ask for pictures, and I was accommodating them because I was so happy. He just sat there watching, eyeballing me. When you're so hot you don't have to speak—that's *hot*.

That night, all these people wanted to make out with me—a hairdresser from Poland, two gay guys. I've never made out overtly at clubs because I have always been afraid the paparazzi would take my picture and I'd be in all the papers. Nowadays, people just come at me! But now I was making out with two women. I started with one, and her girl-friend looked jealous, so I moved on to her. One of them was openly berating the Stallion to egg him on. Maybe that's why he was drawn to me.

Still, he didn't take the bait. But he was looking at me like Sylvester looked at Tweety.

Like I say, it's important to think of something hot when you're se-ducing a man, because it's the best way to send out that vibe. So I was thinking of that *Goodfellas* scene with Ray Liotta and Debi Mazar where he's fucking her out the door. It's the hottest scene in history. We were about to put it to shame.

The Stallion was visibly aroused, and he smoothly suggested we slip back to the VIP room for a little sump'n-sump'n. He was hot, and I was available for action at this point in my life, so I was not against the idea.

But I thought we could do better than a quick hummer in a back room. So I made an excuse and left him hanging, inviting him instead to visit me in my fabulous hotel suite the following night.

He called me five times on my cell the next day, telling me in a sexy Marlon Brando voice, "Oh, baby, I'm so wound up." I told him in a breathy voice, "Oh, baby, I can't stop thinking about you!" (And I had a secret weapon: I'd befriended the concierge, and he told me that if I really wanted to turn a guy on, I should say, "I gots the magic pussy if you gots the thunder and lightning!" This makes no sense, but it's so baldly dirty it's exactly the kind of nonsense a horny man wants to hear. There are words that speak directly to the cock: Learn to speak boner, and you'll get the thunder and lightning, too.)

To prepare, I transformed my hotel room into a boudoir. I don't care if you're in a presidential suite or a house trailer—you can make yourself a boudoir anywhere, as long as you put your mind to it. Here's what I did: I cut the labels out of my cheap H&M panties, and they were instantly transformed into La Perla. I swathed myself in a vintage black Yves St. Laurent and fuck-me stilettos. Then I placed six small white candles on the mantel, and one large white candle in the middle of them, with a black-and-white picture postcard of the Herb Ritts image "Neith with Tumbleweed, Paradise Cove, 1986." Hanging by the fireplace was a spermatozoa-shaped poker (nice subliminal touch). I sprayed myself all over with Diptyque Olene Eau de Toilette—behind the ears, between the tits, at each wrist, and, yes, right between the legs. I was not kidding.

A bellboy arrived, bearing booze ordered ahead of time by the Italian Stallion. "I'm Clay," he said. "That's funny, I'm plastic," I replied. Then the Stallion himself called. "I'll be there in five," he said. "You fuckin' make it four," I growled.

In three, the concierge called to tell me that the Stallion had trotted into the lobby, so I cranked a mash-up of Jimi Hendrix vs. "Drop It Like It's Hot," spread red rose petals all over the bed, and got my camera ready. I'm a fan of dirty pictures. I took a picture of one of my lovers when he was nude—I'd covered his cock in caviar. I know they're not supposed to develop X-rated photos at drug stores, but maybe they made an exception because it was so damn big, or because the caviar took it from porn to art, because I got my double prints with no questions asked.

Mr. Stallion arrived looking gorgeous. I was on a big pink cloud of anticipation as he sipped his champagne and nibbled the hors d'oeuvres I'd ordered for him.

"I'm so charged up," he told me, staring me down. "My thighs are like chicken wings," I said back.

We consummated our affair that night more times than I could count. He started by running me a bubble bath in a circular Jacuzzi. I got in the tub, and as soon as I got into the water he slapped on a condom and got into me. The only foreplay we had, or needed, was that phone call that he was entering the lobby. All he wanted was the image of the supermodel bent over the tub, submitting to him. I looked at us in the mirrors, and not to break the mood, I took a mental snapshot of the position and stored it away for later use in my forearm workout. (Know your angles, girls!) I saw ten thousand images of me in the prisms, hundreds of thousands of little Janices going, "Life is good!"

We looked at each other. A tiny, gentlemanly little bit of drool was just escaping his mouth; he aimed it for my cheek, and I just looked up at him like Juliette Binoche in *Damage*, passively accepting while he wanted to aggressively dominate and fuck.

Because I'd taken the time to seduce the Italian Stallion, I'd been rewarded with the ride of my life.

TIME TO REFLECT

Want to know how to succeed at dating without really trying? There's no such thing. You *have to* try.

Now that you're physically ready—and mentally psyched—for your date, you must consider yourself the Mirror Master. This is one of the absolute keys to dating and relationships. It's about putting out a vibe. Put out the joy vibe, and you'll get it reflected right back at you. Put out the jealous, insecure, mental-case vibe, and the man will act the same way. It's an easy lesson, but true: Your date will mirror your mood.

Just as important, you need to take care *not* to mirror *his* mood if he's being negative.

Let's say you're on a date and it's going . . . just okay. You want to provoke some kind of response. What you should do is decide, silently, that you're going to project a mood onto this man—that you're going to drag him into your world and your desired mood.

Want to set a happy mood instead of the dismal downer of a date you're sitting through? Then for God's sake put a broad smile on your face. Want to get a sexy mood going? Then act like a sex kitten. Sexy's too high class for what you have in mind? Act like a bitch in heat. Pretend your date is looking in the mirror—because you *are* the mirror.

Believe me when I say that this *works*. And trust me when I tell you that the heights of joy can be reached if you set the tone.

When a guy is talking to you, let your imagination run wild. One day recently, as I was getting ready to leave this chic hotel, a bellboy came over to say goodbye. He'd been attending to my needs all week—arranging limos, hunting down lost bags—and he'd grown fond of me. He'd also grown a woodie, which he was sporting in his street clothes as he came over to bid farewell to me in the lounge. Young guy, baby face, but all man. (From Williamsburg—Brooklyn in da house!) He was saying goodbye, but he could barely string two words together. I was imagining being with him on that perfect four-mile stretch of beach at Cabo San Lucas . . . and giving him a little fun in the penthouse.

Dream that stuff up as you're talking, and I promise you the guy will know it. It will conjure up a vibe. I'm not kidding. Go there in your mind, and the look on your face will be his passport to join you.

Act the way you want them to act. If you act nervous, jittery, or calculating, they're going to do the same, whether you want them to or not. And then you'll sit there wondering why this guy is a nervous, jittery, calculating jerk-off. If your date's turning out to be an ass, maybe it's because *you* were an ass first.

(By the way, I'm advising you not to *act* calculating, but that doesn't mean you shouldn't *be* calculating. That's what this book is about. Just don't show it.)

On the other hand, if you reveal some of your vulnerability, he might show some of his, too. He might even take you straight into his heart. And if he does, you'll have yourself to thank—and, of course, *moi*.

Start fresh tomorrow with this attitude. It works in nondating situations, too.

Lesson 9

Late's Not Good for Very Important Dates (or Periods)

TIMING IS EVERYTHING

Women, you know we have a 007 license to be late. We can safely show up fifteen minutes after the starting bell; after all, we have more advance work to do—and we need to create an entrance.

A man must never be late.

If a man is more than fifteen minutes late, he's a prick. If he's more than thirty minutes late, he's probably toxic in every way. Avoid.

What's the longest you should wait?

I hate to dredge this up again, but it's so topical, I'll indulge. I once waited for Charlie Sheen for, like, two and a half hours. He was a total hound dog, but at that time I was single and available for hound-dogging.

I sat at Sushi-Ko on Beverly Glen, waiting and waiting and (this was back in the day—no more!) getting a little lit up.

His shitty excuse for being late? "I was auditioning for *The Green Hornet.*" The movie never got made; Charlie never got laid. (By me, anyway.)

He was so late we didn't eat—see, models don't always starve themselves on purpose. He took me to his limo and said, "Let's split." In the limo, he had twenty lines of blow chopped up on mirrors, so I took my revenge and did an *Annie Hall*, sneezing all over it. (I guess I did screw him after all, in a manner of speaking.)

You know what? I wouldn't care if I was held up by a fucking Lagerfeld fashion show—I would never just drop a name as an excuse and try to get off easy. Fuck you, you disrespectful pricks out there—I'm always prompt. So I made old Charlie give me door-to-door service and watch me walk inside my cool digs . . . without being invited to stay. His reaction was, "Is that it?"

Probably a reaction he was used to getting from women himself.

THE HAVE-A-NICE-LIFE EXPRESS

If timing is important, you'll want to be able to vanish into thin air in no time flat if your date reveals himself to be a jackass.

I know some women find "let's meet there" dates too modern and impersonal, but I don't see it that way. On a first date, you *must* meet the guy at your rendezvous point, because you have to have your car available to split if it doesn't work out. You've got to have a getaway plan. You're like Al Capone—you can't sit with your back to the door, and you can't put your happiness in the hands of some man who could turn out to be a total pig. Unless you have a way out.

Don't let him pick you up. Either meet him for that first date, or stick an extra hundred dollars in your pocket so you have cab fare to go home. Try asking a man for cab fare to flee your date with him. It's not smooth.

THE ART OF THE DATE—IT'S ON

Now that you know how to build up to a date, we're going to have to work on actual dating situations. This date you're about to go on—all that planning and painting and psyching up—this is what it's all been about.

No pressure.

But don't fuck it up.

If you start to panic about doing the right thing, keep this story in mind: I was once having dinner with Princess Caroline of Monaco in St. Moritz, and I didn't know what fork or knife to use. I was hyperventilating. So this classy royal leans over to me and says in a whisper, "Just relax." So simple. So easy.

Just relax.

THE BEST DATE I'VE EVER HAD—BAR NONE

I have to say, absolutely the best date I've ever had was when I was doing a book tour for *No Lifeguard on Duty*. I hope you'll have a date like this in your life—many of them.

I was traveling with a genius of a makeup artist—rather *difficult*, shall we say, but a genius. We fought like cats and dogs on each leg of the book tour—Dallas, Chicago, New York, Miami, L.A., then up to San Francisco, the very last leg of the tour. I was really lookin' hot: The hair was done, the makeup was done. I could feel my chakras ready to burst. I was in Marc Jacobs head to toe—when he was doing slick rock 'n' roll, not that granny kick. I looked fit, tapered, together.

I had a date to tape an interview at an airport hangar with the most popular morning show in San Francisco. So I came out in a rust-colored suit, lookin' smokin'—and here was this guy who looked like a Jewish Jim Morrison (my ideal type). "I bet you've never seen one of these," he said, pointing at the camera. I was like, "Oh, God." I thought he was a grip—a hot Rumanian grip. Turns out he was the interviewer.

I kinda sloughed him off—"Yeah, yeah, yeah, take the picture." Then he did something right: He took me by the hand. I love guys who take you by the hand! He sat me down, and we had that inner connection. He was asking really good questions and making me laugh—humor is key for me. For me to seduce or be seduced, there has to be some kind of humor involved, or acerbic wit, or sarcasm. He was asking amazing questions, and I started getting closer and closer, making excuses to touch his arm, his shoulder, brush something from his face. I was toying with him. He was getting my jokes. I was hugging and playing with him. He was so Aquarius.

He said, "I never do this," and I'm like, 'Yeah, rrrright!" Then he said, "Would you see me?"

I played it like it was a continuation of the interview. "The next time I'll be out is for my book signing." It was at this big bookstore in San Francisco, which I thought was pretty fucking chic—my whole life, what did I ever do? I had two kids, yes; I had hundreds of magazine covers, yes. But if you wanna see me in action, come to my book signing. Being the world's first supermodel wasn't enough, but I bombed at movies, and I bombed at singing. But now I have my books, and my book signings, and my legitimacy. Now I'm Edna St. Vincent Millay.

So I do the signing . . . and the guy never shows up.

Then, when it was all over, he showed up. "Oh, my God. I'm so sorry I was late!"

I cold-shouldered him. "You're late and you're dead. Goodbye—it's off."

"C'mon, I'll take you to the best fish place in San Francisco," he said. "Romance? View?" I love views. Wherever there's a view, I love being on top. So I said, "All right, romance, view . . . I'll do it."

It was midday on a San Francisco wharf. The sky was peacock blue. Alcatraz was the backdrop. Seagulls were doing their "Awk! Awk!" best. I was keeping my chin in the air and looking at him from the corner of my eye, propped up to smooth out any wrinkles. And he just dazzled me. Of course, he was a comedian, and he was doing his *shtick* on me. But it worked. I'm telling you, there was magic in that date.

This led to the best dinner date that evening. As he was driving me back to my hotel in his little hot rod, he said, "This is going so well I don't want it to end." I muttered, "Unh-huh . . ." dangling the keys to my room. But he just said, "Would you like to have dinner with me?" I was psyched. He was keeping me wanting more, giving me a little, then pulling back for later. Take note.

I asked him what he had in mind for that evening. "I'm not gonna tell you," he said. "I want it to be a surprise."

I asked, "What should I wear?" He said, "You'll know what to wear." This man totally understood me. I was feeling this date at the cellular level.

He took me to a comedy club, but didn't tell me he was gonna go onstage. He took me right in, sat me down, ordered some cranberry juice and hors d'oeuvres, and did a thirty-minute set. Hysterical laughter everywhere: He had the room. At the end, as I was still laughing, he said, "I'm dedicating this to my new friend." I stopped laughing. My toes were spreading.

Then he took me to a Sleater-Kinney concert at the Fillmore West. These are all of my favorite things. He knew I loved classic rock 'n' roll; he knew I loved to laugh. He'd read the book!

As we were sitting in the audience, we started making out. Then he took me out afterward for some crab cakes. The restaurant had horrible lighting but it didn't matter; the chemistry was already in place. When we got back to the hotel, he walked me to my room. "Bye, I've gotta go now," he said.

I was like, "Oh, my God!" I couldn't figure out if this fucker had played me or if I'd just had the best date I could remember.

I didn't see him for the rest of the time that I was in San Francisco. But the next weekend he flew to L.A. and checked into the Beverly Hills Hotel—and it was *on* for the next four or five months. It was a great little short-term relationship. And it all sprang from a *huge* first date.

Every date should be like that. It should be fun, and surprising, and full of the art of seduction. Without those things, it's not a date—it's just two people killing time until someone better comes along.

First Dates Are Crucial

GOOD FIRST-DATE SETTINGS

What's the number one stupidest thing you can agree to do on a first date? Unfortunately, it's also the number one most common dating scenario. But resist it. You know what I'm talking about: Never do dinner and a movie on a first date. You don't need to get ignored by a guy on a first date. You don't need to be outshone by some huge silver screen, or by Cameron Fucking Diaz shaking her little white-girl booty all over it.

If a guy asks you to a movie, he goes in the ass category.

Guys come in three categories: the asses, the assholes, and the ass-holders. The asses are silly fucks who don't know any better, but they can be improved. The assholes are hopeless; they have to go. The ass-holders aren't really guys you date; they're not even guys you leave the house with. But they're fun while they last.

If you think dinner and a movie makes a great date, you're only half right. Dinner is fine. But in a movie you can't communicate; you can't be seduced. The only thing that happens on movie-theater first dates is wondering when a guy's gonna take his hand and put it on yours (or your *something*). That move belongs in high school, when no boy with a crush has the sense to string a sentence together. Even if you're already sold on your guy, the movies aren't a great place for making out.

Doorways are better. Cars are better. Hotel rooms are better. Not movies.

On a first date, you need to get to know the person. Movies just take you away to that foreign-jungle, distant-asteroid, planet-of-the-busty-Amazons place. By the time the movie's done, you're so distant from each other you might as well be on an asteroid somewhere—and you'll probably wish you were.

The only girls I know who are happy to take in a movie on a first date are those "Anything you say, dear!" women—your classic passive gold diggers, who'd agree to spend a first date in a sensory-deprivation tank if they thought it would get them somewhere with Daddy Warbucks.

If you want to take in a movie after dinner, wait till about the six-month mark. That's enough time for a guy to get to know you. Anything shy of that smacks of bad judgment—or desperation.

YOU PAY, THEY DON'T PLAY

Who should pay on a first date?

It's simple, ladies: The man. End of story. Janice forgives you your feminist sins.

It's not about who has the power. It's about who's the man.

If a woman breaks out her wallet, she has a problem. Even for the 50/50 split. On a first date, I don't ever want you to say, "What's my share?"

He brought the wallet. You brought the girl. Even trade.

A man who expects a woman to pay half the bill should expect to keep his whole package in his pants all night long. It's just that simple. Paying is a sign of respect. It's a sign that this isn't about friendship. Friends split the check. Lovers shell out the bucks for the women they love.

After all, some of the old-fashioned rules still make sense. I don't care if you're a millionairess and he parks cars for a living; if he's a gentleman, he'll know his place. And no—you can't take care of the tip, or the coat-check girl, or the tolls or taxes. Never, ever, ever reach for money on a first date—unless you're calling a cab to stage a getaway.

Of course, that doesn't mean you should be a bitch about it, and insist your Mr. Parker—Mr. Valet Parker, that is—take you to some chichi place. Make a date for Starbucks, and let him plunk down the twelve bucks for muffins and lattes.

After the first date, the rules loosen up a bit. You pay, he pays—it doesn't matter, as long as everyone is happy, smiling, and well fed. Who cares who gets out the credit card?

And one more thing, girls: Just because a guy pays for a meal doesn't mean you're obliged to offer yourself up as dessert. If he acts like this is expected, tell him you're more expensive than a chicken breast.

Talk Ain't Cheap

GREAT DATE CONVERSATION TOPICS

People ask me, "What should I talk about on a date?" Tip one: Read the damn newspaper. Every morning it's full of plenty of interesting topics. If you're shy, talk about my current favorite date topics (in no particular order): the Supreme Court, Iraq, the possibility of a female president, Arnold Schwarzenegger's haircut, Richard Branson's space mission (could I please have a seat on that shuttle?), the death of glamour, or whatever's hot at the multiplex.

Celebrity couples are great to talk about, because a man's opinion of them can be a very direct line to how he sees himself fitting into a couple in the future.

For example, sometimes I'll bring up Hilary Swank and how *hot* she is with her husband, Chad Lowe. Your date probably won't care about the actual stars involved. He'll just love that you introduced the word *hot* into the conversation. You can tease him and say, "How *hot* is Chad's brother Rob?" (I actually have some juicy Lowe-down stories from my past, but I wouldn't bring them up on a date.)

If your date seems too excited about how hot Rob is, that tells you something right there: Call for the check. And if he knows all the ins and outs of Tom & Katie, Brad & Angelina, and Jessica & Nick, do the same—either he's an undercover gay man, or he spends *way* too much time on an *Entertainment Tonight* intravenous drip.

While we're on the topic of topics, do *not* let the guy you're on a date with go on and on about serious family issues. (And don't you do it, either.) Frankly, if I have to sit through one more date where the guy just wants to tell me how he never got along with his mom and dad, I'll vomit. Please—I had the shittiest upbringing on the planet. If a guy complains too much about his parents, I just say, "My dad was a pedophile. Next topic." I wrote about my issues—I don't try to slip them into every conversation between the appetizer and the entrée. For those stuck in childhood ruts, do not talk about it on dates—unless you're dating your shrink. Replace the whine-a-thon with talk about politics, sex, science, movies, horses, water polo, polio, whatever you want. I just don't want to hear how your father never had any time for you—or I'll tell you I can't blame him.

Nor should you discuss your exes on a date. First of all, it's boring

The ABCs of CBs

What's a CB? It's a cock-blocker. This term refers to anyone who stands between you and the best cock in town. A typical cock-blocker is another woman in the room who's after your man. But it doesn't mean you're necessarily competing for the same thing. Mamas are expert cock-blockers—they don't want you stealing their sons. You can even be cock-blocked by your own children, if they're jealous of any man treating their mother like a woman instead of as the person who gave them life. You must always be aware of potential cock-blockers and be prepared to confront them in any way necessary. When a dog is eating, smart people refrain from attempting to get between that dog and the bowl. Be that dog.

to talk about anyone the other person hasn't met. And you're becoming your own cock-blocker if you talk about past sex partners, even if you don't talk about the sex. A man starts hearing about some amazing cruise you went on with your ex—even if you're trying to tell him you'd like to do the same thing with him—and I promise you, all he can see is a vision of you on your back, legs spread, letting another guy bang you.

I'm also sick of men telling me their ex-wives were more like friends because they didn't like sex. Buddy, did it ever occur to you that maybe she just didn't like sex *with you?*

As soon as a man wanders into ex-land, I have a little trick: I'll bring up something equally boring to him—say, the latest shoe sale at Neiman Marcus. Neither his past sex life nor my present shoe fetish is a good topic. If he's got half a brain, he'll realize the date is going downhill and change the topic. If not, you've learned a little something.

If you manage to get him onto some other subject but then he brings her up again—that spells trouble: He's not over her. Call for the check. If you don't, it'll lead to pain and suffering for you later.

Now, I know some of you think you *want* to know about the exes. Resist! Trust me, you really don't want to know. I don't even want to talk about their kids, let alone past sex partners. Am I a terrible person? No. I have two lovely children, but I don't bore my dates by droning on and on about their latest school projects.

If a guy ever asks you about a past relationship of yours and why it didn't work, tell him: "We spent too much time talking about his exes."

Bonus Points for Presentation

ALL THE WORLD'S A RED CARPET

All right, this is going to sound crazy: You're going to think I'm a micromanager in a micromini. But here goes: When you're walking with your man, you need to insist that he walks in a proper manner.

Don't you hate it when a man drags you through a crowd or rips you through a line at the movies? And doesn't it happen more than you'd like?

You're not a sack of cement. And if he treats you that way, it means he's thinking about himself, not about you.

It's even worse if you have the type of job that means a lot of black-tie events. Recently, at an awards show, my date stepped on my Dolce & Gabbana gown. Gasping, I replied, "Please, take a step back—and get somebody to teach you how to walk a woman wearing a formal gown."

Your man shouldn't yank you around like you're his dog on a leash. If he does, it's time for you to stop walking and let him ask what's wrong.

Then hand him the check.

EVERY DATE IS A "DOUBLE" DATE

In 2005, I attended the Golden Globe Awards dripping in Chopard jewelry and wearing a beautiful black silk Valentino gown that cost more than several homes put together. And the thanks go to Tyra Banks, who was kind enough to poison me for an *America's Next Top Model* shoot.

What do I mean? Let me set the record straight. It's not like we got into some sort of bitch fight and started pouring chemicals down each other's throats. She didn't even spike my mineral water. What I mean is, before we left for that shoot in South Africa where I met the Greek bartender, I was subjected to so many inoculations that my nervous system was basically poisoned. The downside was that I felt like shit for several weeks after I got back to the States. It was not a good time to be on my bad side because I was prone to snapping at a moment's notice. I know it's hard to picture me like that.

But with every cloud comes a silver lining, right? The plus side is that I was able to drop enough pounds to get back to my supermodel fighting weight of my twenties. *Toned* doesn't even begin to describe it. I looked like the cover of a bestselling exercise book (note to self about future project). It was one of those times when you truly felt your body couldn't get much better.

(One aside: I know everyone says I'm too skinny. But I eat all the time. I wonder how many points are in water pills? No, seriously—I just work out to get rid of all the calories I consume. Not that I recommend shots that could kill a horse, but I did feel lean and mean in my Valentino at the Globes.)

Imagine all that black with straps falling softly off my very toned shoulders. I credit yoga—or my brand of it, which I call *Vogua*—for giving me the perfect upper body. *Vogua* is yoga that's designed to make you look like you just stepped out of the pages of *Vogue*. I highly recommend you sign up for a class in your neighborhood. You never know when you'll be getting naked with a handsome man—or even going to the Golden Globes.

You may be wondering about my date for this major Hollywood spectacle. I took my much younger boyfriend, who was thrilled because he'd never attended one of these showbiz shindigs, and longed to walk the walk we all dream of when we're children. Yes, we're talking about the red carpet. I understood how he felt about strolling along the red carpet as a virgin awards-show participant. It took me back to when I did a series of red carpets on the arm of Sly Stallone. Remember him? (Sly, if you're reading this, I'm sorry to ignore you in book three. It's not that you're no *Contender*, but I've devoted enough ink and think to our brief chapter. Have a wonderful life! Love to Jennifer and the kids!)

Here's what I know about red carpets: You don't have to be the star. It's still a major thrillathon when you're strolling half-blind because of the flashes in your face, the cameras poking into your shoulder—and that's not even to mention the other luminaries who are sharing that fantasy rug with you. Gorgeous-people watching doesn't get much better.

That night, my guy looked smokin' in a black Armani tux. We started the evening right—in our limo, sipping mineral water and kissing with tongue . . . which was great but problematic, since it meant I had to keep reapplying my Chanel lipstick. Once our driver deposited us at the event, things started happening very quickly.

After a brusque wanding by very handsome security men, we were on the red carpet. I gave my boyfriend's big hand a squeeze because he looked a little bit nervous. But his feet seemed to be working as we walked the red carpet. It was my own sky-high Valentino shoes that were giving me trouble, sticking in place a bit when I heard the hysteria building up around me.

"JANICE! JANICE!" the crowd screamed. "WE LOVE YOU!"

Which is funny because . . . where the hell were these lifelong fans ten years ago?

Jaded bitchery aside, the waves of love were flowing over me. Right then and there, I decided that we should have an awards show every single night in Hollywood. The world would need a lot less therapy if everyone in the arts could just feel this sort of appreciation. We could even host awards minishows in New York for our friends on Stress Island.

This was no time to worry about saving the minds of those in the arts. When the press swarmed us, I took a gulp, popped an Altoid, and worried a bit about my boyfriend, who seemed to have gone from a little freaked to a lot freaked.

"Janice! *Janice!*" screamed *ET*.

"NO! Come over *here* first!" yelled the E! producer.

"HEY, WE'RE PRODUCING YOUR SHOW! WE NEED YOU *NOW*!" bellowed VH1, my harsh mistress.

This is a wonderful problem to have when you're a TV entity, but when you're a flesh-and-blood famous woman getting pulled in a million directions, it isn't necessarily good for the anonymous man in your life. I stopped for a minute to ponder what he must be feeling. Shock? Pride? Jealousy? There were no answers to be found in my boyfriend's silent gaze. He just stood at my side. Then we took a few halting steps.

I heard a tiny *riiiiippp* and nearly hyperventilated. He'd stepped on the train of my dress. He was literally riding my coattails.

The House of Valentino was being shaken to its foundations.

I had a vision of my entire dress ripping off my body. Well, at least it would have made a great photo op. As it happened, it was just a tiny rip. But my guy went wide-eyed with sorrow and panic. He knew I'd nearly killed the last man who did the same thing. But his eyes! He was too cute and scared for me to hold a grudge.

"Sweetie, it's no big deal," I whispered in his ear. "It's just a dress." Never have I lied better in my life. I wasn't even sure where these words were coming from. I liked this man quite a bit. If he'd been just some half-assed date, I would have probably decked him for stepping on my train. For a split second, I felt a kinship with the late Princess Di. How many of her trains were mauled in the name of walking a red carpet?

So instead I wept inside.

The press, for their part, didn't seem to notice. But soon the beautiful blonde Nancy O'Dell from *Access Hollywood* was in our faces—close enough that for a minute I thought we might make out. She never touched me . . . but she did immediately put her hands on my date!

Whoa! Did she want to be bitch-slapped?

But this wasn't sexual. She didn't want him. She wanted him to get lost.

Touching his arm gently, she said, "Hi—we need Janice alone. Could you move?" That was *Move* as in, "Move your ass, No-Name—*now.*"

Well, this guy is a Leo, so of course he was offended. Sulking away, he stood alone while I did my interview, only to join me again for the last stretch of carpet. We were surrounded by a gang-bang's worth of photographers who were in a feeding frenzy for a hot shot. As both a photographer and a model, I knew they needed to make this quick or they'd lose the great set of tits behind me. Time was definitely money here, and they had no room to move the players around. They just barked their orders.

"Singles! We want singles!" they shouted. Thanks, guys. Were they trying to make *me* single again? My date just stood there, looking bewildered; he didn't understand their lingo. These photogs were starting a dating service on the side—they just wanted me in a single shot. My photogenic date could move his ass. Now, or faster.

There comes a time when your average supermodel must choose between the feelings of the man she's sleeping with and the paparazzi, who have screwed her in other ways over the years. (Note: There are many paparazzi whom I love. You know who you are!)

Was I going to go for my fame or my flame?

"Screw you!" I screamed. "Tom and Nicole didn't stand alone. Brad and Jennifer didn't stand alone. I bet Ellen and Portia won't stand alone!"

Well, maybe I was wrong about Ellen and Portia, who were actually doing their best to keep it low-key with the press at the time. They weren't macking for their own reasons. On the other hand, I had no reason to shove my boyfriend off to the side like he was some sort of off-season accessory.

"I won't stand alone!" I cried. "This is my boyfriend! I love him."

There were reporters around us who witnessed my little show—or should I call it a showdown? They started scribbling notes in a fury; this was better than Cameron Diaz's run-in with the photographers. This was real drama—Janice Dickinson was having a meltdown at the Golden Globes.

To punctuate my point, I hovered over my boyfriend, let my breasts pop just a bit from the dress (an advanced model move you should try at home before taking it out on the town), and even ran one of my diamond-encrusted heels up his leg. Now he was happy—and a little shy at this very public declaration of our relationship. I was giving him my all, and giving the photographers what they needed. It was clearly a win-win situation.

It was a night to remember because I respected my date. Let this serve as a lesson, even if you never get to attend the Golden Globes. Let's say that one day you're at a family wedding or a class reunion. Sooner or later, someone is going to want to separate you from your partner and demand "singles." Your old friends or some ex will want to whisk you away. Just for a few minutes. Your family will need you alone. It won't be meant as anything personal to your date—but you've got to remember, it *is* personal. Another person's feelings are always personal.

If you allow yourself to be separated from the two-pack, your date will have a shitty time and wonder if you really care about his feelings. As for those who want you single, well, it's not their call. It's your call. You can be single for a few minutes at a party, but if you ignore your date, you might be really single later on.

After my public lovefest, my date was in a very happy mood. It got even better that night at the afterparties, when I introduced my boyfriend to Halle Berry and P. Diddy. He pressed palms with Andie MacDowell and posed with all the *Desperate Housewives*. I even met the guy who plays that handsome plumber, Mr. James Denton. I kissed him on the cheek—a harmless showbiz cheek press—and told him how much I loved the show. My boyfriend looked a little jealous, but it's not bad to remind your man every once in a while that there *are* others out there. If he's secure in himself, it should make him feel grateful that you prefer him to all those others. (Besides, Mr. James Denton is married, and his very hot wife was at his side that night. Clearly, I'm not the only one who doesn't believe in singles!)

If He's Got His Eye on the Door, He's Already Halfway Through It

THE WANDERING EYE

When you're out on a date, he is not allowed to flirt with, or even check out, other women. It's not just rude, it's completely *verboten*. (That means forbidden in German and anything in German is ten times more serious than otherwise. Those Germans run a tight ship.)

If your man has a wandering eye, wait until he finally looks back at you and say sweetly, "Can you please do me a favor?" He will lean in and say, "Of course." You reply: "Can you wait until I go to the fucking ladies' room before you start gaping at other broads?"

Do it right and I swear it'll be like you plucked that wandering eye out and fed it to a begging dog. He will respect you for calling him on his bad behavior. If he doesn't—if that wandering eye still makes an appearance—make a point of ogling the male underwear model at the next table and mouth to him, "Call me—I'll be home early tonight."

DON'T YOU FLIRT WITH SOMEONE ELSE WHILE YOU'RE ON A DATE, EITHER, BITCH

I was at this bar, the Burgundy Room, in L.A. and I saw Johnny Knoxville. I was dying because I *love* Johnny Knoxville. I love him more than Jessica Simpson does, and I've loved him longer. But I'd never met him.

And I still haven't.

Johnny didn't see me, because my date and his kid brother knew there was another stallion in the room, so they were cock-blocking him. My gaysian friend Vince was trying to clear the crowd for me. Leave it to Vince to be a reverse cock-blocker (a cock-flocker?). Vince was pinching Johnny Knoxville's ass and looking away; Johnny thought it was me.

We're human. If we're out on a date and see a hot guy, we're going to look. But you can't do it in front of the guy you're presently dating. It's not kosher.

Johnny . . . call me!

Lesson 14

You Can Take It Seriously Without Getting Serious

THE UNBEARABLE LIGHTNESS OF BEING SINGLE

Not every date has to be with a guy you hope to marry. Have fun in the moment. Enjoy a day date. You have no future together? That's hot.

Let me tell you a story. One day, while I happened to be nursing a broken heart, I was pulling into a parking spot by my favorite coffee hangout in West Hollywood when a man in a cherry-red Mustang cut me off. Before I could get upset with his shoddy driving, I looked closer—and saw a young Al Pacino crossed with Vince Vaughn. So why squabble over a parking spot and some illegal swerving? I wanted to merge with this guy in other ways.

Wait—wasn't I supposed to be in the throes of heartache? I'd just ended a short, bittersweet fling; I was supposed to be on a temporary man strike.

Fuck heartache. Why wallow when you can swallow? (Just kidding—a drag queen made me write that.) You can easily move on from all but the biggest heartaches if you just allow yourself to dwell on what's positive and new and not what's old and over.

So Mustang got out of his car in his beige Ugg boots (they were mucho trendy then) and tight blue jeans (always in style with me). On the minus side, the guy looked like a zombie, a.k.a. it seemed to be the morning after a very late night at the clubs. Walking past him, I gave him the J.D. Hizzy, which is a little hip sway and a careful glance back toward—but not exactly at—him. I could be looking at anyone in his vicinity. But we both knew I was looking at him.

Once inside, I took another look and found that Mustang had galloped after me and was standing right behind me in line. Doing a perfect 10.0 hair flip, I glanced out the window at his car and said, "Great car. What a color." He smiled, but I was concerned—up close, his eyes actually matched his ride.

"Thanks," he said. He was hung over, but he wasn't dead.

By then, I wasn't looking at him anymore—but I did overlook my distaste for party animals and give him another chance. Doing a 180, I turned back around and asked, "Who are you? Are you an actor? I want your number; I need actors for my new show."

He cleared his throat. "Uh, I think I'm with UTA."

"You *think*?"

This guy was out of it, and he knew I knew it, which is why he wanted a chance to explain.

"Look, I got dragged to this club called Concord and stayed until six in the morning," he said, looking very sorry about the situation. "Take a little pity on me," he begged. My heart bled.

Then I had a brainstorm: Hollywood is a town without pity, but one thing it's got plenty of is gyms. "Look," I said. "My gym's across the street; that's where I'm headed. First I'm buying you coffee, then I'm taking you to the gym for a shave and a steam."

Mustang looked very amused. "I can buy you coffee," he said.

"Save your money for that gas-guzzler."

A few minutes later, we were sitting together finishing our coffee. Turns out he was a very famous international tennis player from Boca Raton, visiting L.A. on a business trip. He was wealthy enough to have afforded his own spa treatment, but I find that the people who appreci-

Sexiest Treats for Potential Datemates

- FULL SPA TREATMENT, INCLUDING HE-MANICURE AND MASSAGE
- CALVIN KLEIN UNDERWEAR YOU LIKE IMAGINING HIM WEARING
- APHRODISIAC BASKET OF OYSTERS, CHOCOLATE, AND WINE

ate a treat the most are the ones who can easily get treats for themselves. Full-service beats self-service every time.

When we got to the gym (I already felt worked out from our flirting), I gave him a warning. "Be careful," I said. "There'll be tons of gay men popping woodies when they see you."

"I think I can handle myself," he replied.

"That's exactly what you better not do in that steam room."

On the treadmill, I scolded myself. *What are you doing? You don't need a long-distance flirtation—and you can't even play tennis!*

Mustang came out of the steam room looking refreshed and unmolested. If there were any guys around who wanted him, my look said *Lay off: This one's for me.*

Later that day, he dropped by my place and gave me a ride in his convertible. We kissed a few times and promised to keep in touch.

That was when I let myself off the hook. This wasn't an ill-advised long-distance romance—this was a fun afternoon.

As he dropped me back home, he gave me a great kiss goodbye, promising to teach me about love matches someday.

Sometimes, It's the Men !

TOP TEN TYPES OF MEN YOU CAN'T TRUST

It's one thing to turn over some rocks and watch all the men scurry out. The problem isn't that men are in short supply, it's that there are so many men out there who belong under that rock for good.

I've discovered, ladies, that the following men are often *trouble*. I'm not saying that every guy who falls into one of these categories is by definition bad for you. I'm just saying proceed with caution—and don't say I didn't warn you.

Let's examine the most difficult types:

(10) STUDENTS. Yes, they're cute. Yes, they're so earnest. And they're tireless in the sack. But ultimately, they're so young they just don't have much texture to them. And they might be using you for tuition.

(9) COMEDIANS. These guys are nothing but trouble. They're incessantly cracking wise about things that are funny on stage but annoying in real life. They're also tortured artists, the kind who are prone to horrible personal problems. After a few dates, you'll be wishing you were seeing a mime.

(8) POLITICIANS. Been there, done that. You well know who I'm talking about, but I won't get him and his wife in trouble.

If you're wondering whether I mean stay away from Democrats or Republicans, I'd say Democrats. Republicans—I hate 'em, but I date 'em.

Actually, Democrats aren't all great, either. Omarosa is one—in fact, she may be the most embarrassing Democrat out there. Republicans have JonBenet's dad, Democrats have Omarosa. She has one name now, like Cher. Or Lucifer. She's the woman who told me I'm a bad mother on *The Surreal Life*. I wanted to say the same back to her, but she hasn't spawned yet. Still, I bet she was a lousy wife. She's too self-centered and always right ever to relax around anyone, man or woman. I hope her husband got some action on the side. What goes around comes around.

Overall, politicians are bad boyfriend material. In my experience, they're 100 percent fake and 0 percent around when you need them. Unless you have the same burning ambition they do, my vote is a big NO.

(7) BOYS NEXT DOOR. The one thing such a guy has going for him is that he's so damn convenient. Just snap your fingers, and the man down the block or down the hallway will be right there for you.

I have a neighbor we'll call Peter (for obvious reasons) who lives a few doors down from me in Beverly Hills. All I have to do is stand in my yard and whisper, "Oh, Peter . . ." and the guy is on my doorstep like I beamed him over. (Of course, I love standing nude on my balcony; that's my neighborhood welcome wagon.)

It sounds very close and cozy, but the boy next door becomes the pain in the ass next door in the blink of a false eyelash. It's like feeding an abandoned dog—he gets a little, and he comes around sniffing for me all the time. Like, for instance, when I bring home a handsome guy from the beach. *Funny, I don't remember saying, "Oh, Peter . . ."*

The boy next door has also started wondering—loudly—why the beach boy's Porsche is still in your driveway the following morning. None of your damn business, honey.

I've seen all the movies where the woman falls in love with the Tom Hanks type down the street. To those who suffer from such delusions, I say this: If you dump a guy, or get dumped by a guy, and never want to see him again, keep this in mind: The only way to escape the boy next door is to *move*. So make sure your neighbors remain neighbors: six degrees of separation is just about right.

(6) MEN YOU DO BUSINESS WITH. YES, EVEN IF THEY'RE HOT. I'm sorry, but I must insist. You don't shit where you eat, and your business is what gives you the money to buy the food to eat, right? There's a reason I never fucked Nigel Barker, the judge who sat next to me on *America's Next Top Model*. Just like the guy next door, it's a too-close-for-comfort situation. (Plus, in the case of Nigel, the bastard stole every good line I had! And someone else on the show had a crush on him.)

If you shag the guy who works in the next cubicle over—and then suddenly your boss catches on, or the deal you're working on together starts to crumble because you're too busy flashing him your thong, or you date and break up and he wants to get you fired.

The possibilities are endless—and endlessly depressing.

(5) JOCKS. I have girlfriends who have a thing for jocks. I don't get it: For me, it's like flashing back to high school, where everyone wanted to date the captain of the football team. Newsflash: That graduation ceremony was supposed to put an *end* to all that. Yet we're still saddled with those never-say-die jock types who live at the gym even though they're thirty-seven, and after twenty years of lifting they have shoulders so wide they have to turn sideways to enter a room. (And here's the kicker: Lots of these latter-day jocks *never* played sports in high school—in fact, they're school nerds making up for lost time.)

Girls, you all know this subconsciously, but let's face it head-on: For many jocks, high school really isn't over . . . and it never will be.

Of course, there's no arguing with personal taste. If bagging jocks brings out the slutty cheerleader in you, I say *fine:* Go chase them down at the gym and find out how hard their athletic supporters are working.

All I know is that these guys are almost never around for the long haul. I wasn't gonna say it, I didn't wanna burst your bubble—but I've got to throw a flag on the play.

Jocks treat their bodies like machines, so they're used to a quick fuck-and-duck. It's all about taking care of their animal needs, and then it's back to the weights before the abs start going to flab.

By the way, jocks are such a common female fantasy that they're good at getting themselves into trouble. Just look at Kobe. He's married—and his wife, Vanessa, is a total hottie—but he goes for a cheap, one-night stand and it winds up costing him millions. Get it? Even a true hottie can never be hot enough to keep a jock from breaking training with any number of other hotties . . . and even a few notties.

Jocks are not to be trusted. Plus, they'll bring athlete's foot to your shower and leave their smelly jockstraps all over your newly polished hardwood floors. And besides, the jocks of today are prettier than women anyway—Beckham and his type. On *The Surreal Life*, Jose Canseco borrowed my makeup until he looked like something out of the Village People.

(4) BUSINESSMEN/CEOS/VENTURE CAPITALISTS/STUDIO CHIEFS/ENTERTAINMENT ATTORNEYS. I'm lumping them together because these men are all in the same boat. They wear the same suits, keep the same hours, and don't have enough time for you—or any woman. They'd rather make love to their cell phone. At their peak of bedroom ecstasy they're liable scream out, "How many *poooiiints* do I get with that deal?" If you thrive on being ignored, these men won't let you down. If you hate never seeing your boyfriend, he'll try placating you with expensive gifts—which isn't all bad. But it gets old.

If you're the kind of woman who wants her man panting at her feet, well, you better shop around. If a man knows what time the Asian markets open up, he won't have time to open you up.

(3) PLASTIC SURGEONS. More of the same: They just won't have time for you. Ever seen *Dr. 90210*? No? I wonder if his wife has, either.

Of course, just because plastic surgeons don't make the cut as long-term lovers doesn't mean you need to be hasty. With a little nip/tuck to your expectations, it may be worth dating a silicon wizard long enough for him to get you a discount on any freshening up you need. The least he can do is get you in before the holidays—even if his *overprotective* receptionist says he's booked solid. Show him a little skin, and he's guaranteed to have an idea or two about what to do with it.

(2) PERSONAL ASSISTANTS, OR MEN LOWER ON THE FOOD CHAIN IN YOUR PROFESSION. *Hello!* Have you ever seen the fabulous movie *All About Eve?* In the middle of going down on you, he'll be scrolling through your list of contacts and begging you to tell him again about how you broke into the business.

One friend of mine, who's a successful writer, went out with a less successful writer—we'll call him Ron. In the middle of some serious afterglow cuddling, Ron looked deeply into her eyes and said, "Baby, how much did that magazine pay you for your last story?" If she'd had a phone nearby, she would have called me, and I would have given her the right comeback: "Not as much as you'll pay for that question."

Wannabes are a disaster. They don't wannabe with you, they wannabe you! Remember Ron the writer and run.

(1) ACTORS. I've been with lots of actors, so why am I so down on them? Because I've been with lots of actors. They think they're chick magnets, but they're really check magnets.

A while back, the Roulette Wheel of Fate placed me in first class on a cross-country flight next to a cute, dark-haired actor who hails from a family of Midwestern actors. This bookish hunk was ready to party from the starty; as proof, he smuggled a six-pack of beer onto the flight and started drinking before we left the tarmac. The next thing I knew, we were in the mile-high club. This was "prehab," so I was drunk too; I don't remember too many of the details, except that he was hung like a racehorse—a racehorse with beer breath.

It was a very turbulent flight.

"I really wanna date you," he told me when we came down from our high—landed, that is. I agreed, because he seemed sweet, and because he was in a lot of movies at the time.

From the start, though, there were problems. He used to call me at four in the morning "just to talk"—in this weird, breathy voice that might have been sexy if he weren't waking me up at four o'freakin' clock in the morning . . . and if I could have understood a word he was saying.

He wasn't exactly the nicest guy in the world. He had this way of cutting off your words, focusing exclusively on himself. He probably thinks this song is about him, in other words, and in this case he's right. He was also very good at making a woman feel below average in the IQ department, as if that was the ultimate stroke to his very fragile ego.

"I want you to come to Malibu," he whispered one night. I agreed to meet him at his multimillion-dollar beach house, but he was so drunk by the time I got there that he could barely stand. It was a pathetic encounter; from the moment I walked in, I wanted to call for the check. We never even made love. He just wobbled around, guzzling beer and mumbling about the lack of decent roles for someone of his great talent.

I'd driven two hours for nothing, I realized—and with no cash on me, I was out of luck. (If only I'd had this book with me at the time, I'd have made sure to carry an extra hundred with me. Live and learn.) "Do you have a few dollars for gas, so I can get home?" I asked him politely. Who says I'm not a sterling conversationalist?

"I'm not a fucking bank!" he yelled. Who was I—Patty Hearst?

The curious thing is, this actor was as bored with himself as I was. I could tell because he'd been in the process of creating a sculpture made of dollar bills in the middle of his living room. It must have been a very quiet period in his life, because the dollar sculpture went from the floor almost to the ceiling. If I had a dollar for every time a date with an actor took a turn like this, well, I'd own that sculpture.

On my way out the door, I stuck my hand into the sculpture and left with what Clint Eastwood would call a fistful of dollars. This poor fool never even noticed that his sculpture was teetering; he must have been listing at the same angle himself.

TWENTY FAMOUS MEN I LOVE . . .
PLUS HOWARD STERN

Here's a list of real men who make me pant.

Why, Janice?

Don't worry, this is more than just my personal shopping list. I'm sharing this with you because a good way to identify your type of man or men is by making a list of the famous ones you'd drop your thong for in a New York minute. Seeing a list on paper of the guys you go for makes it easier to spot trends. After reading mine, I recommend you do the same—and remember, this is pure fantasy, not a to-do list, so feel free to include dead guys.

I couldn't rank them from one to nineteen, but I'd turn my rig around for any or all of the following. In some cases, I already have.

Warren Beatty.
It's all about his insight—this is a smart, smart man, which is the ultimate turn-on for *moi*. He also played Clyde Barrow, an original rebel, but Warren finally realized that those days had passed and reinvented himself as Hollywood's most loving husband and father. I had him in my clutches when he won an Academy Award for *Reds*. We dated for eight months while he wrote, directed, produced, and starred in that Oscar-winning film. I know you crave dish about the stars, but Warren was always nice to me. In his presence, I could never stop thinking, "Not too shabby, for a Florida pom-pom girl to be dating Warren Fucking Beatty."

And, you know, that could be his real middle name.

George Clooney.

Thank God he's still available. And always will be, because this guy ain't ever committing to anyone beyond that pet pig. But George, I love wildlife—call me!

Ellen DeGeneres.

I love Ellen. I'd eat out with her any day of the week.

Johnny Depp.

He rocks. *Hard.* Once, I took a flight from Miami to St. Barts and ran smack into the devastating Depp with his then-girlfriend, superwaif Kate Moss. They were having a good time in first class, and the red wine rings around their beautiful kissers proved it.

Johnny wasn't the type to insist that everyone leave him alone. I approached him and gave him a script I wrote. Neighbors, right? I said, "Dude, we should hook up. Professionally speaking, Kate." She *did* give me a hard-earned death-ray stare. Johnny didn't care and said, "I know—we grew up around the corner from each other, Janice." (I'm from Hollywood, Florida; he's from Coral Gables.)

To date, that's the closest connection we've had. But the option on my script is still wide open for you, Johnny.

Michael Douglas.

He's insanely rich and has a good sense of humor—something that comes free with recovery. Catherine is a lucky girl.

Eminem.

I love the fact that this guy has the balls to write a song that begins with him vomiting. I was driving around Los Angeles with my son Nathan and we heard that song on his CD. Nathan kept saying, "Gross!" I just said, "Honey, welcome to my world." See, my theory is that Eminem really wrote that puking intro to pay homage to all the supermodel bulimics in this world. Props to Marshall for the shout-out.

Bryan Ferry.

He *is* Roxy Music, the greatest sound of all time. Just listening to this man's voice makes me want to sleep with someone in the next five minutes. And, as if it weren't enough that he can croon a woman onto her knees, he's also one of the hottest-looking guys around. Extra points because he sings my favorite song, "Slave to Love." The lyrics to that song begin this book, and they've defined my life.

Bill Gates.

Ideal man: a CEO who travels. I know being a latchkey squeeze isn't ideal for everyone, but at this stage in my life I wouldn't mind not having to deal with someone all the time. Plus, if I worked it right, I might even get a corporate card.

Tom Hanks.

A solid family guy, and he'd wash your car just because you asked him to.

Josh Hartnett.

Age doesn't matter to me when I'm staring at that expansive, toned Midwest chest. In one of his movies he gave up sex for forty days—but then he never met Janice Dickinson.

Brandon Jenner.

Too young? Isn't that like "too cute?" As in, no such thing?

Michael Jordan.

I'm sure he could slam-dunk me like no other and give me my own label of designer sneakers after he was done. I'd call them Air Sexy Bitches.

JFK Jr.

I know that, sadly, he's left this world, but I still have dreams about him. Why? How can you even ask? Never mind his amazing looks—his mother was Jackie O, who's always been my female role model. I walk around singing "I Wanna Be Jackie Onassis . . ." by Human Sexual Response. No one wore a hat better than she did—except her son, who would run around Central Park wearing all that sweat and a baseball cap. Growl! Plus he was a great, great kisser.

Martin Luther King Jr.

He's quality, and the greatest legend who ever lived. Kudos to Coretta for standing beside him. *Time* listed him as one of the Top Five Americans of all time, but I'd give him a little something new to march for and rank him number one.

Tommy Lee.

Still one of the hottest rock stars going. I saw his porn video, which I like to think of as an audition tape. His cock looks like something you'd see on a farm. Sometimes you have to climb Mount Everest just because it's there.

Jon Lovitz.

I know what you're thinking, but I'm serious—he's simply the sexiest man alive. It's all about his humor and his insight. And he's a real-life twin, which is very alluring. I'm available to be his dream girl anytime.

Steve McQueen.

He starred in *The Great Escape*, but I wouldn't want to escape Steve McQueen in his prime. It was a war movie where handsome, sweaty Steve was stuck in a cell, insisting he didn't give a rat's ass about his plight. *That's* a real man. He just sat there bouncing a ball against the wall and didn't let the bastards get to him.

There are other reasons to love the late, great legend. He raced cars and spent time hanging out with Jim Morrison. Cool and cool. Every single time I drive by Laurel Canyon and Mulholland, I think of Steve.

Stern Taskmaster: Is Howard Good in Bed?

Is Howard Stern good in bed? It's a question that used to keep me up at night.

I couldn't decide if he officially made my list or not. On the one hand (pun intended), Howard is always talking about pleasuring himself, which made me wonder if that's all he ever does.

When I did his show one time, Howard asked me if I'd had sex with anyone the night before. "Yes," I said defiantly. He said, "With who?" and I wouldn't say, so he called me boring. So I said, "I pleasured myself." It's not even a phrase I normally use; I just said it because I knew he wanted to hear it. Howard likes masturbating so much he gets off on hearing about other people with similar inclinations.

I used to wonder if he banged that hot girlfriend of his—and that, in turn, made me wonder what kind of lay Howard Stern could be. Just as often, though, my mind would wander to his beautiful girlfriend and I'd think, *I'd rather do her than Howard!*

Does Howard make her happy? I'm skeptical. He probably just lies there and she does all the work.

If he ever had a round in the ring with the Big Dog, I guarantee I'd still be walking around afterward and he'd be flat on his flat ass begging for mercy. I'd rate his skills in my next book and call it *Public Parts*.

But Howard will never get that chance; I've stopped wondering about him. The last time I did his show, he tore my tongue out of my mouth. As soon as I arrived, he called me an "old model." Honey, the only difference between some ugly old stringy-haired beast and Howard Stern is a radio show.

Sorry, Howard, but you're off my list. Check, please!

Hell, if I'd been in spit-swapping distance back then, I'd have done a threesome with him and Ali McGraw. She was pretty handsome back then, too.

Ryan Phillippe.
Young and so hot—plus, it's a lock that his wife will be out of the house at any given time.

Steven Spielberg.
He could easily make me a star. Oh, did I write that out loud? But really, that's not the *only* reason he's the perfect man. It's just the main reason.

Tiger Woods.
It's a pity that that woman he recently married beat me to the punch. He's young, sexy, and rich. I thought he might be the One. He's got a little of every race in him, but I bet he's black where it counts.

FIVE MEN I'M FRANKLY A BIT SICK OF THESE DAYS

I'm not saying these guys are not good lust fantasies for some of you; I'm just saying . . . enough already. I'm over them. Check, please!

Jose Canseco.
I spent twelve days locked in a house with this baseball legend and I never saw his bat. No wood in sight. Plus, he used my lip gloss more than I did.

Lorenzo Lamas.
I heard he walked out of a screening of *The Aristocrats*—a fabulous movie where every comedian in the world tells the dirtiest joke ever invented—because he couldn't take it. Anyone who can't sit still while Bob Saget swears is a big pussy and not dating material.

Jude Law.
He's packing in as many films as he can before he loses the hair, not realizing that he lost it some time ago.

Bronson Pinchot.
I still have no idea who the fuck he is, but he's got bad manners and no chance in hell of getting anywhere with the Big Dog.

Brad Pitt.
Familiarity breeds contempt, and contempt just breeds—he's a bit too all over the place for my taste. Brad . . . call me, and we'll go away together, somewhere *far, far away.*

BLIND AMBITION

I know you want me to be more bold, as in the boldfaced names. Every supermodel finds herself on the arms of men who don't need introductions. Right now, you're thinking it's one of the perks of the job. It can be—until you realize that famous men are even better at breaking your heart than regular Joes.

Some are just amusing and give you funny stories to tell.

I'm thinking of the late, great Ray Charles. Several years ago, I was invited to go to a musician's lunch at the Bel Air Country Club, where Mr. Music Legend was an honored guest.

As a longtime fan, I made a beeline for him. "Hey, Ray," I said. "I'm Janice Dickinson. I used to be married to a musician and—"

He wouldn't let me continue; he simply reached out and took my hand, just the way Jamie Foxx did in the movie *Ray*. For a blind guy, he had great aim—and it wasn't limited to hands. Ray was a grabby guy; in a split second he was touching my waist, and drawing my butt down to plant it right on his lap. I know he used to sing about "no peace I find," but he seemed pretty good at finding a piece.

I have to give it to Ray. He was a man with a mission, and got me right where he wanted me.

He didn't even speak, which was very sexy for a change. It made me anticipate hearing his famous voice for the first time.

"Mr. Charles," I continued, lap-trapped, "I'm here with a date. He's a bass player. He's a hunky blond man. You're going to have to release me or he'll get jealous."

Ray smiled and whispered in that raspy voice, "Janice, you remember 'Georgia on My Mind,' don't you?"

Of course, I told him I'd played it around three million times.

"Well, Georgia ain't on my mind today," he chuckled. "Janice is," Ray said. I know a famous man's personally branded pickup line when I hear it—and usually I know enough not to take them too seriously. I was on Ray's mind because I was on his lap.

Ray may have been a musical genius, but he was also a hound dog. Pulling me closer, Ray actually stuck his tongue in my ear.

I said, 'Whoa! Ray, uh, Mr. Charles, I think something else is on your mind, too."

In the end, Ray kissed my cheek. Sweet. He also tried to stick that tongue down my throat. Kind of gnarly. But still, pretty good aim for a blind man.

I later learned that this was vintage Ray Charles—he was quite the ladies' man. A musician who got laid all the time? Who would have imagined?

But I didn't feel any kind of karmic connection with Ray, and I don't think you should fool around with someone just because he's famous . . . unless he's famous for his Apollo Moon Rocket.

RYAN SEACREST: METROSEXUAL OR TOTAL PUSSY?

I'd like to take a minute to discuss how I called the nonromantic check on boldface name and former talk show host Ryan Seacrest.

You may have read something about a little squabble that we had last year while I was promoting my second book, *Everything About Me Is Fake . . . And I'm Perfect* on his former show *On-Air with Ryan Seacrest*.

The Big Dog has remained quiet when it came to Ryangate because

I didn't want to stoop to his level (literally—he's short) at the time. When it comes to the topic of extricating, though, I can tell this story and kill two birds with one stone, so I will.

Fiction: I jumped in his lap and tried to go down on him on the air. Are you kidding me? Are you *On-Drugs with Ryan Seacrest?*

Fact: Before we filmed the show, a line producer hired by Ryan's production company came to my dressing room backstage and said, "Janice, please be flirtatious with Ryan."

"Like Mrs. Robinson and Benjamin Braddock?" I replied.

The producer nodded and smiled. "First, Ryan will talk about all the men you've slept with," he said.

"All of them?" I said. "I may need an accounting firm to step in and verify the tally."

"After you've talked about the men, pretend to flirt with Ryan like you're coming on to him as your next guy."

That was the setup.

Fiction: Ryan was startled by my antics on his show.

Fact: No, girls: Ryan just always has that startled look.

It was Janice who was startled—from the moment I saw the shitty lighting on this show. After working with Miss Tyra Banks, I know great TV lighting—and I made them change the bulbs to flatter both Ryan and myself.

Boy Host was grateful, but he was also his usual nervous self. As taping time approached, his nerves grew: The Big Dog was apparently something of a threat, and Ryan's more like the Little Pussy. Suddenly, it was time to roll—and Ryan began by comparing me to Courtney Love.

I just ignored this babble; instead I focused on his shirt, which had a small ketchup stain. Without warning, I jumped in his lap, bent down a bit, and started rubbing the stain off. He treated this as if I were about to go down on him.

Ryan, honey, I don't know if you have a lot of experience getting blow jobs, but if that's how you think it works, you're not doing it right.

Ryan was stunned; he looked like he'd just been shot. So did the FCC; they yanked me! Fade to black; I was extricated from the show.

At the time, I couldn't even be upset about it. My mind was filled with one thought: "Ryan Seacrest is a very sloppy eater."

In the end, it was a pity that Ryan had to pretend to the press that our little encounter wasn't preplanned. Don't believe the hype: He was neither shaken nor stirred by it. I even heard that the next day, he placed a call to his good friend Simon Cowell from *American Idol* to diss me. Simon's reply: "I think she's the hottest thing on TV. Can you get me her number?"

I guess Ryan didn't want anything messing up his boring banter on the show—which might be why America has voted and it's no longer in production. The guy can't speak if it's not on a monitor, while I'm a summa cum laude when it comes to improv.

Grow up, Ryan—it was just good TV. And get a new dry cleaner.

A SPECIAL SALUTE TO MAMA'S BOYS

I dedicate this section to the entire nation of Italy.

Like Jewish men, Italian boys have the mama's boy thing covered. It doesn't matter if you think you're the center of their universe. You're not. They'll forget you in a split second when it's time to remember Mama. If you're dating one of these Italian Stallions, you know what I mean: *You don't cook like Mama. You don't clean like Mama. You don't realize the value of a buck like Mama.* Chances are, the one reason you're there is that you do realize the value of a fuck—which is the one thing Mama could never provide. Remind them as much as possible: It's your ace in the hole.

As a mother myself, I know what it's like to love your son with your entire heart and want only the best for him. Wait, I'm rereading that sentence and it sounds so lofty. Here's what I mean: I don't want my son to be at the feet of just any mean bitch out there. But I keep my feelings to myself, because I don't want him to turn into a mama's boy.

I don't want him saying to potential dates, "My mother is the world's first supermodel, and you show up with chipped nail polish?" (However, in such an emergency I *would* advise my son to call for the check.)

The worst mama's-boy story I've ever heard concerns the man who postponed his wedding day because Mama needed him to come over that weekend and paint the outside of her house. When he moved in with his fiancée, his mother secretly pulled her to the side and told her, "Only sluts live with boys." Her son was forty-two years old, and this "slut" was a nice pediatrician who was beloved in the community. She was too busy saving children's lives to be a slut.

Whenever they tried to go on vacation, Mama would call that morning with her endless array of life-ending illnesses—hangnails, slivers, mysterious migraines, and her always-handy fake sinus infection, which seemed to be progressing into a brain tumor. That's one mean, manipulative mother, if you ask me. You don't tell your child your health is failing unless you've just dialed 911.

On the other hand, there are mama's boys out there who come with amazing mothers. If his mother takes you shopping at Prada and says, "Honey, it's on me," then you know you're dealing with the Gold Card of parental units.

One of my marriages was ruined because I couldn't handle the mother. She was rude, mean, and dismissive of me, to the point where I never showed up at any family functions—which, it turned out, was exactly what she wanted. That way, she could spread the word that Janice was "too good" to hang out with the rest of the family. Honestly, I couldn't win. When I did show up at the odd family dinner, Mama would spend hours reminiscing about my husband's childhood and how she'd had "such high hopes for the rest of his life"—words she spoke, of course, with a mournful gaze in my direction.

I would like to call this woman out by name in print once and for all, but there's no point—and the lawyers won't let me.

Girls, it's a universal rule: You can't get between any man and his mother. You cannot say anything bad about your man's mother—not even if she's an axe-wielding serial killer with the type of Florida-red hair that went out in the seventies. To your man, she's a strong woman, the feminine ideal, and she raised him. He will never forget it, even if he isn't really that nice to her himself. He might tell you he hates his mother's guts, but the second you agree he'll hate you forever.

Ways to a Boyfriend's Mother's Heart (If She's Semi-Sane)

(5) READ TO HER. She'll love it, whether you're reading her the *TV Guide* or her favorite cat-lover publication. Bring her your celebrity magazines when you're done with them, too—she'll come to associate you with excitement. (Of course, I try to make sure I'm not in them before I hand them over.)

(4) BRING HER CHOCOLATES—AND TELL HER SHE CAN AFFORD THE CALORIES. If she has a sweet tooth, mine it. If she prefers salt to sweet, some nice paté will make her feel spoiled. (Just make sure the paté isn't spoiled, too.)

(3) TAKE HER FOR A WALK IN HER WHEELCHAIR. A spin around the mall will go over big. Don't leave her in the middle of the street somewhere.

(2) LISTEN TO BORING STORIES ABOUT HER TRAVELS. As excruciating as it is, force yourself to ask to see pictures. Ask to see more. Bring a bullet to bite.

(1) TELL HER YOUR BOYFRIEND'S EX WAS BEAUTIFUL WHEN SHE SHOWS YOU PHOTOS. And she will.

What if his mother says something nasty to you—say, "I loved my son's last girlfriend, but he ended up with you." Put on your game face; act as if you might even like the old bitch. Smile at her warmly and say nothing. If she tells you that you'll never get her son to marry you, smile again. Say nothing. Give peace a chance. Go Kabbalah on her ass. She's obviously trying to work your nerves. Don't take the bait; do not engage in her rage. She'll make it a million times worse, turning on the fake tears and telling her son how you hurt her feelings when she was "just trying to be nice to her even though everyone thinks she's not right for you!"

"But Janice," you may be thinking, "I want to *poison* her. She's old. She had a nice life. Can't I crack her in the head with a big brick?" Step away from the Home Depot, ladies, and put down Exhibit A. If you kill her, you can't count on appearing before a female judge whose boyfriend's mother hates her, too.

You're not allowed to dismember Mama, but you *are* allowed to call your best girlfriend the next day and tell her how you wish the old bitch would drown in her bathtub. You can live a rich fantasy life—it'll cheer you up.

When you're tempted to say something bad to your boyfriend about his mother, though, it pays to stop yourself cold and think, "Could anyone say anything mean about *my* mother that I would agree with?" If his mother is truly heinous, my best advice is to avoid her at all costs. You can also try killing her—with kindness. Buy her candy. Bring her cards and trinkets. When she goes on the attack, ratchet it up a notch, and turn yourself into the sweetest woman in the world, even it if means sending yourself into a diabetic coma. Why? Because then the mother will have nothing on you. She provoked, but you revoked her plan to turn you into monster megabitch. That's her way to get rid of you. Don't be gotten rid of.

We are all fear-based individuals. She's afraid you're taking her boy away. You are. Just be smart about it.

Lesson 16

You Set the Rules

RAISING THE BAR

Before we go further, let me tell you a little story with a moral to it that you might find helpful the next time you start dating a man who comes off as controlling.

An all-American blond named Kelly was sitting on a barstool at one of the hippest clubs in NYC. I was riding shotgun.

It was Saturday night, deep into summer, a time when all you want to do is strip off your clothes, crank up the tunes, and let your fake hair fly out of an open car window. The problem is, it can't be just *any* car.

Jake owned the windows on the kind of car an all-American blond would look great hanging out of; he also happened to own the bar stools and the floor and the drinks everyone was gulping like water. He was six foot five, with curly, dark hair; a sweet face; and bright blue eyes, and he looked construction-worker cute in his blue button-down cotton shirt, white sneakers, and Levi's 501s. He wasn't *L'Uomo Vogue*, but *Sports Illustrated* works for some guys. He was also effortlessly funny, smart, and clearly smitten with Kelly.

Kelly wouldn't normally make out with the bartender, but Jake wasn't a normal bartender.

In my cultural-anthropologist role, I watched them mack in the corner, wondering if he had an investment partner who might have a little better fashion sense. But I digress—this isn't about me. (Oh, my God, it isn't, is it? I don't know if I can bear to go on with a story that's not about the Big Dog, but in the interest of presenting the dating dos and don'ts of our insane times, I'll force myself to shift the spotlight for a hot minute.)

After their public makeout session, Kelly and Jake did something totally wild—they started *dating*. Jake even lost his slouchy jeans—get your mind out of the gutter, though, this isn't about sex. Not yet.

One night, Jake stared deeply into Kelly's eyes and said the words that all women long to hear. No, not "I love you" or "Marry me." This was even better: "I want to take you away to Belize for a vacation."

Kelly had herself a handsome man who was gainfully employed and had great taste in dining. (Even if he'd never heard of Armani . . . enough, Janice, let it go!). Sounds perfect, right?

There was only one glitch. Kelly was at that point in any new relationship when a girl often feels the need to . . . fuck things up.

We've all been there. Let's face it: You really do want to leave them before they can leave you, but—I caution—don't do it *before* the vacation to the tropics! Timing is everything, and geography is pretty important, too.

But she wasn't fucking things up *blindly*. Kelly had been developing a gut feeling. There was something in the way Jake seemed to slide her around like a mug of beer on a bartop. She felt he was trying to control her in every way—and what better way to control her than by dragging her along on this vacation?

"Why don't we just go to a movie?" Kelly suggested, pooh-poohing the vacation to an island paradise.

He rebounded firmly. "No, no, no! Forget the movie," Jake insisted. "Look, I really want to get away with you. And we're going to go scuba diving together. It's *my* favorite thing in the world." He was sharing a side of himself and spoiling her rotten all at once. Or was he really just attempting to do whatever he wanted and to hell with her feelings?

Kelly had only one problem with this plan—it's called drowning. She'd never scubadived in her life, and she figured she couldn't oxygen-deprive herself for very long; after all, as a model she was on such a strict diet she could barely stay conscious on land, let alone twenty thousand leagues under the sea. Cutting her hair, changing the way she dressed, quitting smoking—it was all hard to do, but she knew she could handle it if the right man asked her in the right way. Fucking up her lungs and having her bloated, dead bod discovered on the beach—that was *not* happening.

"Well, getting my nails done is *my* favorite thing, and you don't hear me asking you to do that with me," she reasoned. She might have been a model, but all women are lawyers on some level.

Jake blew up like a lung with the bends, confirming Kelly's instinct—major control freak.

Ladies, we've all been blind-sided by control freaks, but there's no reason for it to happen more than once. The only way you're ever going to be happy is if you're the Big Dog in your relationship. You should be the one who's a Pandora's box of surprises. You need to be setting the pace. You need to be the mistress of your own destiny. It's about controlling and not being controlled.

It's not easy, but it's possible. Make it a goal.

Lesson 17

Dates Are Made to Be Broken

HOW TO ESCAPE THE DATE FROM HELL

We all go into a date with a feeling of optimism, I think. Dating is the ultimate example of positive thinking: "Maybe I'll hang out with this new person and discover we're soul mates and I want to see him again and again and again."

Doesn't always happen. Sometimes you show up and the guy is all hands, bad manners, gross breath, self-centered, boring. These are all hanging offenses.

I know it seems drastic, but you must be prepared to ditch a date. Back in the days of Studio 54, I left a coke dealer during our date. I saw Iman walking across the room, and told him I needed to go say hello. My spiked heels walked right past her and out of the place.

The dealer called me all night long, screaming that he was going to "slice me." It was easier to ignore him on the answering machine than in person. "Don't you know who I am?" he yelled. But by that time, I had my overnight lotion on and was reclining in my bed.

You're never under any obligation to continue a date that's a disaster. One must always have some RFR revved up to deal with a disappointing date. Here are a few choice ways of escaping. Some of these are good for ending not only a date, but any chance that he'll ever call for Round Two.

If the dud date is already at your home, it can be harder to extricate. One strategy: Go into your fridge and find a food product that's about

Top Five Great Escapes

(5) "DID I MENTION THAT I'M PREGNANT AND LOOKING FOR A FATHER FIGURE FOR MY CHILD?" If the man still expresses interest after this . . . all the more reason to call for the check.

---

(4) "I JUST HAD A ROOT CANAL." Translation: "This date makes me feel like I just had a root canal." Or: "I'd rather be having a root canal." Either way, he'll get the message.

---

(3) "OH, MY GOD, I LEFT A CANDLE BURNING IN THE BATHROOM WHILE I WAS GETTING READY FOR OUR DATE! MY HOUSE WILL BURN DOWN! I MUST GO!" I did this one once—and when I got home realized I *had* left a candle burning.

---

(2) "MY UTERUS IS FALLING OUT." Or, for variety, you can always substitute *placenta*. Variations: "I've got cramps," "I've got my girlie," "My ovaries are blocked," "I think I'm starting to get hemorrhoids," "I just popped a varicose vein very close to my inner thigh." Anything amiss in *that* region will gross them out, and make them suggest, "Maybe you *should* go home." If necessary, feel free to go more drastic: "Oh, my God, I think I feel another cold sore coming on. What is *wrong* with me?"

You may wonder if he'll ever call again if you use that last one. He'll call.

(1) "THIS ISN'T WORKING. CHECK, PLEASE." I tell it like it is. If you can handle it, the direct approach is always the best approach. You just cut your losses and leave.

to expire. Take it into the bathroom on the sly, then return to your date a few minutes later with faint smears on your shirt. Insist that you're sick with food poisoning, but tell him he's welcome to nurse you through it all night long if he wants. At this point, fake a heave and watch him go for his car keys.

Another home option is to go to your bathroom . . . and never come out. In your own home, you'll always win the waiting game. Just stay put, treating it like your panic room, until he leaves.

The bathroom is also useful for extricating yourself from a painful restaurant date. Just call a cab on your cell from the john, and then slip out. He'll realize how toxic you two are together if you're willing to ditch him so dramatically.

By the way, if you're already sleeping with someone and just want to ditch him for a night or two because you're legitimately sexhausted, it's best to let him down gently. Simply say, "My labia and I need time to regroup. We thank you for understanding."

I know a model who went on her worst date ever with a boring screenwriter. This was a man famous for earning $5 million a script. He invited her to have dinner with him on a Saturday night at the Ivy; it all sounded very promising.

For an hour, we planned her perfect outfit and thought of witty things she should say to a man who put words in other people's mouths for a living. Mr. Scribe picked her up in a huge white limo, handed her the requisite dozen roses—and then proceeded to talk about himself, and how great his career was going, at endless length. He topped it off by mentioning that he really had little time for anyone else in his life, and that his past girlfriends generally got upset because he had to ignore them for months on end.

By the end of this boring evening, he thought that he'd earned an invite up to her condo. Yeah, nothing makes a woman wetter than a self-absorbed guy with an airtight schedule.

She agreed to let him come over, knowing that she would be getting rid of this moron in record speed. When they got there, she made the hottest honey lemon tea known to man. Pouring the scalding liquid into a cup, she handed it to him with a warning.

"Don't get burned. It's hot," she said.

Of course he ignored her; his words were the only ones that mattered. A sip and a second later, he was coughing out his tea.

"I warned you," she said.

"I wasn't listening!" The hot tea had the desired chilling effect on the date. He retreated to the limo.

The next day, he had the nerve to leave her a voice mail chastising her for being rude to him.

She wasn't home. After he left that night, she'd called a man from her gym and they'd met up for an early breakfast.

Fade out.

HOW TO MAKE YOUR FIRST DATE YOUR LAST DATE

Yours truly, the Oracle, went on a date with Scotty Caan. Yup, that's right, I went out with Sonny Corleone's son. Scotty's father is none other than James Caan, who got shot up when he pulled into that horrible toll booth of death in the longish movie classic, *The Godfather*.

Scotty is James's son, who starred in the teen football movie *Varsity Blues*. He's a wild kid, though he barely came up to my chin. One night we were at a club, and the kid was acting pretty charming. We danced, we hung out, and he kept whispering in my ear, "Let's do it! Let's do it!" He wasn't talking about finding a cure for cancer or putting together a peace march.

On the way to his house, I had that instinctual, never-ignore-it feeling that I was making a mistake. When we pulled up on his drive, I silently counted about a hundred reasons that I needed to get out of this—including the fact that I couldn't wear any of my Manolos around this small-fry. In the end, I kissed Scotty, and told him he was a great actor, but I couldn't imagine a life with no heels. I'm a woman of stature; my man needs to measure up.

Just bringing up the topic of height got me out of making a mistake with Scotty: He was insulted enough that he turned around and drove me home right then and there. But it was better to insult him on the first date, before we got involved. If I'd done it later, I might've wound up with a horse's head on my pillow.

Which, in all truth, might have been preferable to Scotty Caan.

If you want to call for the check decisively, be honest. It never fails.

MEN WHO TREAT YOU LIKE TOYS

The other night I had a date with this guy who owns one of the hottest restaurants in Los Angeles. He looks like a young, secular Mel Gibson, which was one for his side.

I spent three hours at home getting date-perfect, including the three Ws: washing, waxing, and wearing the sexiest wrap dress and black spiked heels. Donning about a million bucks' worth of jewelry (all of it given to me after modeling shoots) completed the look, which could be described as "expensive perfection."

The limo arrived at my house at 9:00 P.M. with a sweet note and a dozen white lilies. He couldn't come with the car, since he was working, but wrote that he was counting the minutes until I arrived. Nice!

This is what happened: I strutted through the front door of his eatery, and he wandered over to give me a quick kiss and an appreciative once-over, like he was the fashion police and I was a model citizen.

Satisfied that I'd put in the effort, he paraded me around the restaurant.

For almost two hours.

It was like he was a little boy at show and tell. I was the show and he was there to tell everyone about how we were suddenly dating each other.

Do you know how exhausting it is to do laps around a restaurant in

Jimmy Choos? I should've worn my Keds. My feet were screaming when I finally insisted on sitting down, ending this dog-and-pony show.

Once I sat down, he joined me and decided to engage in a public display of kiss, kiss, kiss.

"I just want to show you some affection," he said.

"Why don't you show me an AmEx Black Card?" I said.

At this point, a waiter appeared and my date tried to shove some rolls at me. Please! Did he have no consideration for my feelings? I'm a supermodel. I'm bread-shy. That's like handing a diabetic a candy bar. Carbs may be good for the face, but BOTOX does just fine. I watched a model at the table next to me spit some of her steak into a napkin, and we exchanged knowing glances.

I heard her tell her date, "The calamari was delicious."

Spit, spit, spit.

"I ate three crackers earlier today—I'm good," I told my date, who had ordered me a salad with celery so stringy it was like eating fishing line. I excused myself to hit the john, where I could get the stuff out of my teeth; I figured he'd probably called ahead to make sure there were paparazzi lined up outside to catch us after dinner.

The bathroom was a pathetic scene of girls doing coke and taking pills. Some were dancing in the john and two women were grinding and making love to each other near the sink.

The spitter was in there, too. "I guess we have to go back to our dates," she lamented.

The minute I got back to the table, my man tried to stop me from sitting down again. "Do you want to walk around again?"

Obviously, the tables had turned over; he knew there would be a new crop of gawkers needing to see this guy with his outrageous super-model. He didn't want to waste a minute of the walk of fame with me. But that was *so* not happening. My feet were killing me. They hung in there just long enough for my final walk—out the door and straight into the limo.

"Let's get out of here quickly," I said to the driver.

My restaurant friend called that night, and for the next few, wanting to know what went wrong. Could he honestly have been that stupid? This man had no interest in getting to know me. I was just a trophy on his arm for the night—a common dating situation. He takes you to a party or an event, and then makes sure everyone knows you're with him. Your feelings about this are the least of his considerations. It's all about pumping his ego.

Put his ego in check by calling for it.

WHY MAN'S BEST FRIEND IS BETTER THAN MAN

Last year, when I put down my beloved Labrador, Bruno, I was so heartsick it was like breaking up with the love of my life. Bruno (named after my former flame Bruce Willis) was one of the major relationships in my life. He survived forty thousand of my romantic relationships (his head made good Kleenex), an IRS audit (with all the attendant fear and stress), and two childbirths (with all the requisite screaming). Dogs are the most devoted pets on earth. I couldn't dream of existing not having a pet.

Why are dogs better than men?

Dogs are loyal. Men are fickle.

Dogs don't leave you when you get a little older and have a few lines. Men do.

Dogs will follow you anywhere. Men won't—some of them expect you to follow *them*. Which is a huge mistake.

Dogs don't care if you're in couture or an old T-shirt. Men do.

Dogs don't measure your worth by the size of your bra. Men use cup size like a reverse elementary-school report card.

Dogs hate strange pussy in the neighborhood. Men love it and covet it.

I could go on and on, but here's the most important point: Dogs don't need you to play shrink, nurse, maid, whore, gardener, or light bulb screwer-inner.

One night, an erstwhile lover of mine was reclining in bed after getting the most awesome sex of his life when the bulb on the nightstand lamp blew. "Honey, can you screw in the light bulb?" he said diffidently. "The extras are in the closet."

What was I? The help? "I might be Polish," I said, "but I'm not your maid." Then I went downstairs, where Bruno was waiting for me (I'd brought him along for the night). I grabbed his leash, and quietly we slipped out for a walk. All the way home.

I think Bruno was happy that I'd called for the check. And my dog was certainly warmer than the man I left in his cold, dark bedroom.

The Phone Is Your Friend

CALL WAITING

If your date goes well (or well into the morning), in no time flat you'll be wondering about your future together. You'll be waiting for some kind of sign. You'll want him to pick up the phone and call you.

Wake-up call, ladies: He is *not legally required* to call you the morning after a date or after getting laid for the first time. Of course, it's nice—but how often in this world are people nice? You still have to wait it out and let him call you. If you call him first, then he's not nice and you're not smart.

When he hasn't called you for three days, become your own best friend and stop yourself from calling him. Throw his number away. Or call your nearest gay friend and whine to him. He knows men are assholes. One gay friend of mine asked me recently, "Janice, am I just your pet homo to call when your boyfriend's dissing you?" Isn't it wonderful how our gay friends understand us?

Yeah, I knew he'd eventually call. If he finally calls on Thursday for a Saturday night date, say yes. Life's too short and so is my attention span. If he calls on Saturday afternoon, you can still go out with him on Saturday night—if you're free, and you want to see him. It's called *being spontaneous*. You can sit around at home for no reason at all instead, I suppose—but to me that sounds like bullshit.

If you're trying to avoid calling a guy you've made up your mind you shouldn't (like a married guy or an ex), keep yourself busy. I eat stupid all-carb meals, or watch dumb romantic comedies like *The Wedding Date* with that hot Dermot Mulroney. (He had a twenty-four pack in that—and he's back on the market, girls!)

It's better than being all hung up on a man I know better than to call.

PART II

Advanced Dating Techniques

Never Date Below Your Standards

THE BIG DOG GETS PUNK'D

I got punk'd one Friday night last winter on VH1's *BSTV*, which is all about celebrities being lured onto fake reality shows. Mine was called *Speed Dating*, and it was an updated version of the vintage *Dating Game*. I wasn't surprised when my agent got a call asking me to be the choosee on what I thought was a real show.

The deal was, I got to sit on one side of a screen while four male contestants tried to woo me with their sexy voices and witty demeanor. All I can say is, these men had no idea what they were in for—because, as we've already established, I'm not easily impressed.

The first voice presented his vitals to me: "I'm a four-foot, eleven-inch Jew, Janice." He had a nice voice, but when he stopped right there, I realized he thought he'd be getting the hook right away because he basically came up to my crotch. I like Jewish men, but I don't like short guys, so that was a draw.

Ladies, if I've learned one thing over the years when it comes to dating, it's this: Focus on the positive. And don't slam them immediately for something completely out of their control. Imagine telling a blind date over the phone, "Hi, I'm a CEO, brilliant and sexy, but I need to drop fifty pounds." And then the man replying: "Oh, so you're fat?"

"Oh, you're Jewish," I replied (focusing on the positive). "I like Jewish men. Just ask Jon Lovitz." Now it was my turn to ask my midget man a quick question. "Should you and I eventually find out we have hot chemistry and then get engaged, would you ask me to convert? Would you ask me to make matzoh ball soup? You know, I don't really cook—kosher or not. I don't discriminate. I make reservations."

Shorty was speechless for a minute. Finally, he replied, "No, you wouldn't have to convert. Or cook! These wouldn't be problems."

"That's good," I replied. "Years ago, I told one of my husbands that I'd convert, and I never really did. In case he's listening, I'm sorry, Simon."

Number two was a guy from Seattle. A *big* guy. "Janice, I'm a 250-pound black guy, and tonight I'm dressed in a blue suit. You could say I'm black and blue."

Oh.

A sense of humor.

A bad one.

For once, I didn't really know what to say. "I love those colors," I blustered. "Although I should make it clear right now that I'm not into S&M."

A decent recovery, I thought. Only problem was, the big guy didn't get it. (Could it be he was also a blond?) He didn't even fake a laugh, which meant that he wasn't focusing on the positive.

"I'm ready for man number three," I breezily announced. In TV terms, this was the on-air, dating-show version of "Check, please!"

The next contestant was another black dude named Brandon. I thought it was odd that half the panel was black. What have they heard about me?

"Hi, Brando," I purred.

"I like nicknames," he purred back.

"Tell me about your ideal date. What would you do with me?" I said with maximum wide-eyed innocence in my voice. (It's called *acting*.)

Brando didn't hesitate; clearly, he was a man who came with a plan. "Janice, baby, I'd take you for cocktails. We'd go out to eat and have a few more cocktails. Then I'd take you back to my hotel room where we could have another cocktail."

It was time for me to interrupt.

"And then you'd try to fuck me because I'd be so drunk?" I asked. By now, my wide-eyed tone was gone, replaced with disgust. Over-indulgence and rehab'll do that to you.

The producer of the show was obviously disgusted, too. I guess I wasn't supposed to say *fuck* on the air. I'm sorry, but sometimes no other word conveys the same vibe.

But Brando didn't miss a beat. "Yes, I'd take you back to my hotel room to fuck you," he replied smoothly.

By now the producer was waving his hands in utter shock. It was one thing for me to say *fuck*, but now it was a virtual fuckfest and they were going to have to bleep both of us because this was too good to do another take. Plus, it was supposed to be a "live" show, so all the bleeps would give them away.

I couldn't worry about network standards or censorship, though; I had bigger fish to fry.

"Hey, Brando, let me clear something up for you—you're wasting your cocktail money on me because I don't drink," I said. "So I guess the only way you could convince me that we should fuck is with your personality—and clearly you're not that intoxicating either."

"I wouldn't date a model anyway," Brando retorted. "Or a business-woman."

"Well, then I'm out on both counts," I said. "But let me ask you a question. Why won't you date a businesswoman? Obviously, you could never handle a model."

Brando let that one just bounce off his thick head. "I just want a regular girl," Brando replied. "I want to buy my girl a big house, but I'll expect her to clean it. I don't believe in maids."

By now, the show was so out of control that I couldn't stop sticking it to Brando. "Well, I'm out again. These hands have never seen the pole of a mop," I replied. "I'm also allergic to scrub brushes."

Sighing, I motioned that we should move on. I didn't need to go another round with this macho moron.

I had questions now, but not for the men. What I had were those silent, rhetorical inquiries that I keep to myself, such as: Did the show save the best for last? Was the final contestant my guy? Did they want me to compare him with the previous three choices to realize that he was a good guy? Could it get any worse?

The answer to the last question was yes.

Man number four said hello, and then launched into a heartwarming little story.

"Ya know, my best friend is in prison for killing his girlfriend. But the bitch deserved it, because she cheated on him. I don't want to go that route," he told me.

"He . . . *killed his girlfriend?*" I said, choking.

"He killed her live," he replied.

"What does that mean?" I asked in horror.

"He locked her in this box and didn't feed her or give her much air. She died," he said with no emotion.

"Oh, anything seedy about *you* that I need to know?" I asked. "Besides your taste in friends?"

What followed was a long pause. It was as if he were deciding if we knew each other well enough to give me a few inner secrets about his life.

"Well, Janice, once I had sex with my mother. But just once. We were experimenting," he said.

I was speechless.

"I hope that's not going to be a problem?" he asked sweetly.

"But what if we go to your mom's house and she wants a threesome?" I joked, desperate to rescue the whole absurd thing with some levity.

"That's okay with me," he replied, quickly.

"Well, my father was a pedophile, so I'm out," I said.

At this point, a big-busted hostess flew across the stage to gush about the entire evening. It was time, she said, for me to make a decision. Which one of these men would be my love connection? My soul mate? My date *du jour*?

There was only one answer. "I'm going to pass on all four," I said.

I'm not sure who gasped louder, the hostess or the four losers.

"I have a hot boyfriend," I said. "He is not cheap. He doesn't expect me to clean. He doesn't sleep with his mother. But I'm grateful for your kind invitation to appear on your show. Thank you very much. And good luck."

They would need it—the luck, I mean.

The next female up to bat was ready to take my spot in the hot seat. It was Traci Lords, the former porn star turned tell-all author.

Passing Traci on my way backstage, I whispered to her, "Maybe you'll have better luck, honey, but I doubt it."

"Janice, how bad was it?" she said, looking quite concerned.

"You're a woman of taste, Traci. Just remember that," I advised.

Backstage in my dressing room, I paced like a caged animal. How in the world could they have subjected America's first supermodel to such a parade of losers? Were these people crazy? Was that the best they had to offer? Should I leave the country to find a better crop of men? Could dating really be living down to its reputation?

"You were punk'd, Janice," said a producer who stuck his head into the dressing room.

"Punk'd?" I retorted. "They didn't punk me. I didn't choose to go on any date." I definitely didn't see Ashton Kutcher around.

"We made them losers on purpose to see how you would handle it," the producer said. "You were punk'd."

Taking a second to reflect, I calmly replied, "Well, you paid me. So

I guess the joke is on you." I was punk'd on a knockoff of *Punk'd*, but I made money doing it. I always say that if you get a chance to do something strictly for money that doesn't conflict with your values, why not do it? I have kids to put through college.

On the way home, I picked up my young boyfriend and we had dinner at the Four Seasons in Beverly Hills—and we put it on the show's tab.

RAISE YOUR EXPECTATIONS, NOT YOUR SKIRT

Sometimes it's hell finding Mr. Right instead of Mr. Yeah, Right!

The other day, I heard a horrifying story from a friend. She had just lost fifty pounds and was ready to get back on the dating scene after a two-year absence spent making love to a Twinkie every night. (Talk about safe sex—no risk of an STD from that creamy white filling!)

My friend was rusty on the horrors of the dating market, so she decided to check out a popular Internet dating site to slowly shift back into the fast lane. She's always been a very beautiful girl; now, without the weight, she's a knockout. But no matter how hard we women work to improve ourselves, though, we tend to retain our worst moments of low self-esteem more stubbornly than we retain water. In her brain, she's still riding the full-fat gravy train and bouncing around her house in sweatpants.

Her vestigial low self-esteem is why she passed over all of the really good-looking dudes on the dating site ("What if they're disappointed in me?") and did something I find truly offensive.

She lowered her standards.

Instead of point-and-clicking on men who were good looking and had bucks, she decided she wasn't worthy of their approval. Instead, she chose a blue-collar guy with an extra fifty pounds of his own and a love of motorcycles. Let's call him Jed.

Don't panic. I have nothing against blue-collar men if that's your thing. Many of them are great, stable, hard-working men. But they need chicks who really appreciate the idea of washing the grease out of their jeans. I'm also not against guys on Harleys. (The extra fifty pounds, I'm not such a fan of, but that's my own issue . . .)

Anyway, my friend is the kind of girl who loves shopping at Barneys; the only way she'd ever buy a motorcycle jacket is if Cameron Diaz was wearing it in *InStyle*. And even then she'd never wear it on the back of a hog—she'd walk down Fifth Avenue in it, wearing a pair of fresh-out-of-the-box Manolos.

After she sent him her picture and stats, Jed called her to set a date. He sounded reasonably nice, she tells me. The only problem was, they had absolutely nothing in common. My friend is a Hollywood publicist; Jed worked on cars. I know it could be exceedingly romantic, in a Bruce Springsteen sort of way, but even she admitted that on the phone they had literally nothing to talk about—at least, once they'd settled whether her car had a V6 or a V8. The only V8 in my friend's life was the veggie juice she used to lose the weight.

Despite this major red flag ("We have nothing to say to each other!"), she set a quick coffee date and called me with her fantasy plan. Obviously, he was going to be hunky; his extra pounds would make him brawny and not fat. (Uh-huh. If TV adds twenty pounds, the Internet adds a hundred.) Perhaps she could learn to love motorcycles. (Uh-huh. And I could get used to shopping at Wal-Mart.) And he might be truly impressed by her Uptown Girl attitude. (Or would the whole thing play out like *Christie Brinkley and Billy Joel: The Sequel?*)

"Hopefully, he'll be freshly showered and not smell," I offered helpfully. She was not amused.

My lovely, slim friend met Jed—and it was *so* not love at first bite of coffee-shop croissant. First of all, she didn't eat much; he ate three French pastries . . . because he was—surprise!—*fat.* His rolls hungeth over distressed, mid-eighties-style jeans. But that wasn't the worst part; what really bothered my friend was the fact that Jed seemed bored when she talked about her busy life. She was much more polite when he spent half an hour talking about fixing his old Mustang.

"Have you ever worked on a car?" he asked her.

She brightened. "Once, I actually found the hood release so my ex-boyfriend could replace the windshield wiper fluids!"

Jed was not impressed. He ordered a chocolate chip cookie to wash it all down.

This story wouldn't be so bad if it ended right there, but it didn't. My friend swore to me that she had no desire to see boring old Jed again; she was sure he didn't like her either . . . which is why she was shocked when he called a few days later to inform her *why* he didn't like her.

"I only like girls with long hair," he said. "And I think you're a little bit full of yourself. You don't need anyone in your life, and I need to be needed." Once that settled in (or after he'd had a chance to swallow whatever it was he was eating), he continued. "Plus, I wasn't attracted to you," he said. Finally, the ultimate blow. They all use it. It's the dating equivalent of WMD—the Weapon of Masculine Dolts.

A classy girl to the end, my friend didn't do what the Oracle might have under the circumstances—that is, tell him: "The only woman for you, Jed, is Sara Lee. But then again, she's rich and famous and that might bother a loser like you. She might end up telling you the same thing I'm telling you: Eat me!"

Instead, my friend hung up in tears and called me in full meltdown. If even low-class lowlifes didn't like her, she feared, how could she ever attract a decent man?

"You have to stop and collect yourself," I told her. "First of all, this man knew you'd never go out with him again. He was not in your league."

"Then why did he say all those ugly things?" she cried, still not getting it.

"He was groping for ways to hurt you, because you're doing better than he is and he's jealous," I said. "He issued a preemptive strike. It's just that simple."

I suggested that she do a couple of things. First, I told her that she should never lower her standards again. It's not worth it to date a guy just because you think he's beneath you and he'll be an easier ride—because he'll be just as hurtful, and when he's threatened by you he'll be sure to turn on you as soon as he gets a chance. Being rejected by a reject is *much* worse than being rejected by a hottie. Why not save your energies for guys who are at least worth messing up your mascara for? If you're lucky, you might mess up your lipstick *with* them instead.

Second, I told my friend to go out and buy herself a bouquet of eleven white roses with one red rose in the center. Then, she should make it her job to keep the roses as fresh as possible, so they could live a long flower life. Before the red rose died in the center, I told her, her assignment was, at the very least, to cultivate an interest in a man worthy of her. It didn't matter if he reciprocated. She just needed to apply herself. Perhaps she could go out with this new man, or simply work on getting a first date. Even just flirting would count.

This would help her get over Jed—or, more to the point, get over the big, greasy blow he'd dealt to her ego. Without a new love interest to distract her, she'd just obsess—which just sucks, as we all know from experience.

Besides, there's one other risk you run if you lower your standards: If you set your sights on a lousy guy, you might actually end up getting him!

In Praise of Younger Men

AGE IS JUST A NUMBER

Remember Soccer Dad? Things never did work out with him. Just when I finally thought we were getting chemical, he broke off our little meeting, slapped me on the back, and said, "See ya next game." Like I was Rusty the water boy or something. Can you picture anyone smacking me on the back? I don't love to be touched unless I've given permission, and I never like to be smacked.

Worse than the invasion of my space, and the forcible shaking up of my chi, I couldn't believe it: Suddenly I thought I'd lost my touch. Was the Big Dog ready to be put down?

Then this pimply-faced seventeen-year-old kid came up and stared at my ample décolletage. In a voice breaking with hormones, he said, "Miss Dickinson, I just wanna say, too bad age is just a number." He had the phrase backward. And he probably wasn't any more capable in other departments. But there he was, staring at me with this big ole boner. And for a moment, I thought . . .

The moment didn't last that long. My age was one number, a prison sentence was another, and subtracting the second from the first would have made a really unpleasant number.

Besides, I didn't really find the idea that appealing. I can't do the Mrs. Robinson thing. I can't be the MILF. I can't be Stifler's mom.

But when you're worried about your numbers, there's nothing that can make you feel better quicker than someone with a lower number checking out your rack. It was a sweet moment, really, not at all like a *Lifetime* movie. I promise.

In reality, many of the men I've dated seriously have been in their twenties. A lot of the examples I'm using in this book relate to men who are younger than I am. But so what? I don't go after young guys on purpose, and they're not guys who only want older broads. We just connect. If you meet a guy who's older or younger than you are, consider the age difference, but worry more about your virtual ages. I can be fifty and look and act and feel twenty-five, and be dating a guy of twenty-three who acts like he's forty-eight and a half.

Age is just a number. Virtual age is what it's all about.

Men know this; they just think it only applies to them. One time, a boyfriend's grandfather hit on me. He was ancient, but he was the one who made all the money for their ultra-rich family. One day, when his grandson—and his wife!—were under the same roof, he cornered me in the hall of their mansion and he said, "My plane is out on the tarmac."

That's all he had to say. I just melted. But that zillionaire grandfather was also a serial cheater, and I didn't want the bad karma. I ignored the grandfather's passes.

Besides, I'm not sure I could do the Anna Nicole thing. I don't have the right disposition for court.

Lesson 21

Take Two—They're Cheap

JUGGLERS DON'T JUST WORK AT THE CIRCUS

Is it possible to be involved with more than one guy at a time? The answer in my book is, Hell, yes. Are you kidding me? Happens all the time.

I call it mandatory juggling.

We live in a world of multitasking. As I dictate this, I'm having a mani/pedi. I can triple-task, but that's only for the very advanced classes.

When juggling dates, you can often convince yourself that you're in love with both of them. That's to be avoided.

Once, I was dating two guys at the same time, and I had a habit of taking them both to these particular restaurants I loved. Problem—I got simultaneous phone calls. I was on a date with one . . . and the other was in the bar one restaurant away. "You wanna join me?" he said. When I pieced together where he was, I was spinning. *Eat fast, Janice*, I thought. *Eat fast and get out.*

The secret to multidating is, you can't let one find you with the other. Even if they know the score, they don't want to see another guy in your presence.

Juggling two men isn't always the same as outright cheating. You may be juggling because each man is incomplete as a whole, and together they fulfill all your needs. Once I was dating a man who gave me security and a future, but he was terrible in bed. At the same time, I had late-night dates with a smokin' actor who wasn't into tomorrow, let alone a future, but who was hot enough in bed to give me the attention I craved on that level.

You have to realize the risks when you juggle, because if the men find out, you might end up alone. Until they do, though, stop fretting about it. Everyone in the world has done this at one point. If you have one boyfriend, and then fall hard for a guy you meet on a plane, you're not really falling in love with another guy—you're falling in lust. Whether you give in to these lustful cravings is up to you.

Years ago, I was dating a dashing CEO who took me to a sushi restaurant one night. After a few sips of sake, I realized that the sushi chef was hot. (God, don't get me started on Japanese men.) I didn't roll with the sushi chef, but I thought about it. He had his pluses—including the idea that I'd save money catering my next dinner party.

When it comes to juggling two men, you must weigh the circumstances. Can you keep your main man and get in and then out of a quickie affair before he notices? Or will he find out and dump you? Do you love the man you're about to cheat on? Is it worth it? How are your hormones doing when it comes to the other man? Are they rocketing out of control? Do you think the other man could be a potential partner? And do you really think I could hook up in the long term with a sushi chef? Is there enough Bulgari soap in the world to get that smell off his hands?

But all good things must come to an end. I have girlfriends who never do anything about the second guy; they just waste thousands of hours dwelling on the idea of juggling two men. In my opinion, this is the worst possible scenario. Don't waste your brain power this way—because while you're dwelling on the maybes, you're ignoring the first man. He's bound to lose interest. You could end up with nothing and no one in your life. The key is to weigh the circumstances and make a *fast* decision.

Listen to what your inner voice tells you.

You think I'm telling you to cheat? Well, let's look at the international situation. In France and Italy, it's an acknowledged way of life that many men have wives *and* mistresses. I know a man who sleeps in the city of Paris five days a week at the house he bought for his model mistress. On Friday mornings, he makes love to her one last time, kisses her goodbye, and then goes home to his wife in the country house they've owned for years. And that's not just the French: I know one L.A. studio CEO who bangs his secretary around 10:30 every morning after returning his phone calls, then tells the secretary to make a reservation for him and his wife at the Ivy for lunch. There's a model friend I know who loves to screw male models in her dressing-room closet before each of them hits the runway. Once she's strutting around on the runway, she always gives a wink to her millionaire boyfriend, who never misses a fashion show.

The problems crop up when your secondary crush or B-list lover takes things too far and doesn't respect the rules of engagement. A while back, I was dating someone when I met a hot skateboarder. Hot Wheels and I macked a bit, and I told him I'd do what I could to see him once in a while, when the time was right. But he didn't accept the rules; he started calling me all day—and, worse yet, all night, even when my boyfriend was staying over. I had to make up all sorts of excuses to keep the boyfriend from catching on.

I asked Hot Wheels to stop. I even told him I wasn't a phone person. But he couldn't control his dialing finger.

In the end, I had to break all ties with Hot Wheels and threaten him with the idea that if he ever called me again I'd come over and smash his skull with his own skateboard. About twenty-five calls later, he finally got the idea.

Moral of the story: B-list boyfriends can easily turn into stalkers, because all too often they'll be the ones you're ignoring. And you know what I've told you about ignoring men—it makes them all the more interested, even when that is not the intent.

What's the solution? First, rent the Mike Nichols movie *Closer*. Here's the setup: Jude Law is dating Natalie Portman. On the side, Natalie is also doing Clive Owen in the strip club where she works. But both men fall for an independent and gorgeous photographer played by Julia Roberts. They love her for one reason and it's not her bod. It's because she tells the truth even when the men don't want to hear it. And therein lies the secret to juggling men: You must tell everyone the truth.

Julia tells the men she's doing both of them. They don't like it. But they know. They respect her honesty.

Meanwhile, the much younger Natalie never tells her boyfriend Jude about what's going on with her and Clive. Why can't she? Because she hasn't yet become a grown woman. As a real woman, you should be able to look a man in the eyes and say, "Yeah, I cheated on you. It was good. You don't pay enough attention to me. Don't like it? Check, please."

Excuses When the Phone Rings in the Middle of the Night

- "IT'S MY SISTER." NO ONE CAN QUESTION LATE-NIGHT FAMILY CALLS.
- "IT'S A MODEL FRIEND—SHE'S STRUNG OUT." BECAUSE IT'S SO CREDIBLE.
- "IT'S UNICEF ASKING ME TO BE THEIR SPOKESPERSON." IF HE ASKS WHY THEY'D CALL SO LATE, TELL HIM IT'S MIDDAY WHERE THEY'RE BASED, SOMEWHERE IN AFRICA.

Lack of Consideration Begs for the Check

TEXT THIS

I hate text messages. They're so fucking impersonal—a total turn-off.

Once, after we'd spent a wonderful, naked night together, a man text-messaged me: "how r u doing?" This was obviously a true romantic; I can only marvel at how long it took him to craft such a heartfelt, complex sentiment. You know, if it isn't hot and sexy enough to make it into, I don't know, a collection of *Great Love Letters Written to Janice Dickinson*, then don't write it. And if you have to write it, how about paper? Good old papyrus, baby. Put hand to paper for Janice!

If a man dares to text you—unless it's something urgent, or you're in junior-high biology together—refuse to answer this type of no-effort effort.

Later on, my guy texted: "y r u ignoring me?"

Not really. I was just putting in the same effort he was: None.

The next day, after a slew of begging text messages, I finally wrote in big letters: "WE HAD SEX. I THINK U CAN CALL."

He called. "I know we had sex, Janice," he said. "But you don't have to break out the capital letters. It seems like you're screaming at me. There's no need for screaming."

There was no need for text messaging, either.

I called for the check by simply saying, "I'll text message you later." I tell no lies: I later texted him: "NEVER CONTACT ME AGAIN."

Live by technology, die by technology. There are no special effects in romantic comedy.

SHITTY GIFT GIVERS

Ladies, I can't emphasize this enough: If your long-term man doesn't give great gifts, then call for the check immediately. I know this makes me sound very materialistic, but, hell, I am.

The truth is, though, I'm not all about *expensive* gifts. A good gift has to show thought; it should reflect how much he values you. If your musician boyfriend writes you a rock anthem, that counts for more than when your billionaire boyfriend hands you a Dooney & Burke bag, even if the bag is amazing.

My sister once dated a guy who seemed sweet and charming, but deep down I just knew he was a cheap bastard. The proof was under her Christmas tree, where he plunked down a big box.

Along came Christmas morning and my sister snuck out of bed with her new boyfriend, who was actually excited for her to open his gift. I can just picture my poor sister getting her hopes up and ripping off the ribbon . . . only to see the words Crate & Barrel. I'm sorry, but if it comes from Crate & Barrel, chances are it doesn't scream out "romance." She was shocked & disappointed.

The cheap asshole gave her a set of four wine glasses. I'd estimate he spent about forty dollars. Me? I would have dropped that box of wine glasses on the floor—accidentally, of course—and smiled when I heard them break. Then I would have broken off our relationship and taken all the breakage—including the guy—to the curb.

My sister did the right thing and dumped this guy. It runs in the family.

My rule of gifting from men is simple: If you're in it for the long haul, buy jewelry. If you have the cash, it better be jewelry with carats. If you're broke, the only other acceptable gift is lingerie.

Simple. Direct. And the same goes for both major occasions and smaller ones along the way: It's all about the clasps or the straps.

Recently, I carried on a minor flirtation with a major tennis player. One day, he came over and said, "Janice, you've been so nice to me. I'd like to reciprocate."

"Reciprocate with what?" I asked.

This guy was cool; he knew the answer. "Reciprocate with carats."

This was a real man. This tennis pro had balls.

If your guy is a keeper in other ways, but he's crapping out in the gift-giving department, you have to show him what you like if you plan to stick around. The only solution is to grab his credit card and go on a spending spree. I don't care if you take the cash out of the food budget and serve him Special K for dinner. What price can you put on a major life lesson like being a good gift giver?

Order the good stuff and have it sent to your house. Don't open it when he's not home. Leave that for when you're together—and pump up your glee when you open the packages. He'll decide one of two things: Either you have a secret admirer, or he blacked out one night, went on the Internet, and ordered the stuff for you himself. If you convince him that he bought it for you, take him immediately to the bedroom and show your gratitude. It's like training a dog: He'll begin to link good treats for you with good treats for him.

No one is immune to the shitty gift giver. A man once gave me a vacuum cleaner as a gift. Of course, this was many years ago, so maybe it was his secret way of telling me I was doing too much blow. Still, I called for the check before I was even done unwrapping it. (The vacuum cleaner, on the other hand, I kept for years.)

Women are always asking me about the best gift I've ever gotten from a lover or husband or admirer. That's easy: Mick Jagger once gave me a brooch that completely filled the palm of my hand and was smothered in fat rubies and huge diamonds. I slobbered over it. It was

Big Box = Big Disappointment

A large box doesn't usually signify a great gift. If the box is too small to be a Lexus and too big to be a diamond bracelet, chances are that its size is just compensating for the tiny impact it's going to have on you when you open it.

my first piece of major fucking jewelry. Then, a few nights later, I lost it at Studio 54 and I was in tears. Talk about leaving your cake out in the rain. Picture me in my Halston pantsuit and glitter eye shadow, sobbing uncontrollably.

I called Mick. "The most terrible thing happened last night!" I sobbed.

"What is it, Luv?" he said.

"I lost the brooch you gave me for my birthday!" I wailed.

"Girls!" he said with a sigh. Then he added the words that still sting to this day: "You know, you could've bought a house with the money I spent on that brooch."

Of course, in that situation it was Janice who was in the wrong, not Mick. And he's no shitty gift giver. But ever since I heard those words, I have *hated* when men tell you how much they spent on your gift. You shouldn't be told how valuable a gift is; it should be fucking obvious just by looking at it.

I decided to get over the brooch and Mick. Tomorrow is another gift.

Keep It in the Closet

WHAT'S HOTTER THAN FRANK SINATRA?

I once had a date with a European prince named Leonard Rabinowitz. It was a setup thanks to our mutual acquaintance, Tony Peck. (Oops, did I mention that Tony is Gregory Peck's son? Oops, did I mention that Tony is the godson of Frank Sinatra? Oops, did I mention, he's also the friend who was most responsible for getting me sober, and that he has the most gorgeous child on earth, named Zack Peck?) Again, I digress—though it's not my fault; it's just not often that one amazing male sets you up with another fabulous find. When the universe throws this sort of handsome karma in your direction, it's only right to go with the flow.

But back to my prince. As soon as he called and I heard his slightly nasal voice on the end of my cell phone, I knew I was in luck. You shouldn't immediately start looking into your crystal ball on the first date—it's better to just take stuff as it happens because you might be pleasantly surprised. In this case, though, it was hard not to project ahead, since I knew Leonard had a reputation for taking care of the special lady in his life—and I have a reputation for liking to be taken care of.

And I don't just mean being "taken care of" with credit cards. Or jewelry. Or fabulous trips to Europe. Or designer clothing. Leonard's rep was based not on all such standard rich-boyfriend perks, but on one gift he'd given his ex-girlfriend—a gift that made resculpted jawlines hit the asphalt of Rodeo Drive.

Leonard built his live-in love a $300,000 closet in his home.

I know. Take a moment. *Digest.*

On the night of our first meeting, where I was going to be his date at an intimate dinner party he was throwing, I drove to Leonard's marble palace of a home atop a bluff in Beverly Hills, knowing it held a closet I basically wanted to move into for the rest of my life. (I'm not even kidding. Give me some food, water, and grooming products, and I would sell my home to live my life in that closet. Besides, are you kidding? Living in the closet in Hollywood, I'd fit right in.)

"How do you even *spend* three hundred grand on a closet?" I kept wondering as my BMW SUV FU2 lurched up the hill to his home. After I was buzzed in and the gate opened, my mind drew a complete blank when it came to clever things to say to Leonard; I just kept trying to figure out how many shoes you could fit in a $300,000 closet. Was there a butler in there on twenty-four-hour duty? Did it have a mini bar? Its own mayor?

"Janice, how lovely that you could come," Leonard said, gallantly opening the two-ton oak doors for me. No wonder he needed a personal trainer—just letting people in was like doing the rowing machine at the gym. In person, he was a blond prince type, early fifties, with zero percent body fat and two helpings of smarts. He was the brains behind Carol Little, the fabulous designer. He actually used to be the stud behind her, too, since they were married, but it's cool—they had one of those rare friendly divorces (better than an unfriendly marriage). Maybe she was the one who taught him about closet space; little did she know how effective that would be later, when it came time for Leonard to score pussy galore.

If you build it, supermodels will come.

So there I was, standing in his lavish foyer. We kissed lightly. Then he said the words to me that every woman in Beverly Hills longed to hear: "Would you like a tour of my home?"

Does a billionaire want a prenup? I was *dyyyyyying* for a tour.

I could bore you with the details—the marble floors, the crystal chandeliers, the furniture that was imported from everywhere on earth. But this isn't HGTV. I could describe all the well-appointed men and women mixing and mingling in his swank digs, but if you've seen one heir or heiress, you've seen them all.

"I have an interesting closet," Leonard said. Nice. Cuts to the chase—bonus points.

"Really?" I said casually. "Wanna share? If you feel comfortable, that is." Of course, if he hadn't, I would have induced comfort by knocking him out with one of his antique lamps. One way or another, I was seeing that closet.

My Manolos closed the gap between his bedroom door and the closet in a Hollywood second. Leonard tugged open the doors (another workout) and . . .

I was used to climaxes in bedrooms, but nothing compared to this knee-knocker.

This closet was like a well-appointed estate in the East Hamptons. Remember, he'd built it as a present for a girlfriend who left him, but when she left she couldn't take it with her; after all, it was part of his house. Advice, girls: Anyone receiving a $300,000 closet from a man should try to make a go of the relationship.

Of course, a closet like that is an invite to fill it up. It's a gift that keeps on giving.

As the Chanel gloss drained off my lips, I saw a rack for the seventeen Valentino gowns this bitch owned—and *left* in her ex-closet. On another side of the closet were shelves for enough shoes to choke Barneys. There were drawers for the most high-end jewelry I ever salivated over, bar none. Diamonds, emeralds, pearls in all shapes, sizes, and forms—Candy Spelling would have been in awe.

Leonard knew taking me to his closet was a huge mistake; after a few minutes, I was measuring it for drapes. But he was the savvy type; his contingency plan was a little more subtle than simply picking me up and carrying me out of there over his shoulder. He actually lured me out with a pound of Beluga caviar and an ivory spoon. He also upped the ante with a promise: If I followed him out of Closet Nirvana, I could meet the guest of honor that evening: Frank Sinatra.

Ol' Blue Eyes pushed me over the edge.

At dinner that night, I pondered: Better to stay in a closet fit for a sultan, or lock eyes with the legendary leading Rat in the Pack? That closet was pretty powerful, but with Gregory Peck and his wife rounding out the table, soon my mind was wandering.

A few glances into Frank's baby blues pulled me into focus. Frank twinkled each time I looked his way. At one point, the legend leaned over and said, "Young lady, I think you're pretty hot." Sadly, Barbara probably sensed her husband's harmless interest and began to cock-block me. It was truly unnecessary—Frank Sinatra was not about to pick me up. Though I did have an intense Ava Gardner thing going on.

That sent me back to the closet. I should have locked Barbara in that closet! She could have lived there happily; then at least I could go back to flirting with her legendary husband.

On second thought, I had no interest in disrupting the Sinatras' wedded bliss. For me, the only conquest I was interested in that night was the one I could never have: a deep and profound relationship with Leonard's closet.

Rules Go Out the Window with Old Flames

REDATING

Not for nothing did God put billions of men on the planet. We're not supposed to date one and then go back for seconds and thirds. When it's over, it should be over—or it shouldn't have been over in the first place.

Would I ever break my own rule and date an ex? I have to give it serious thought, because if—*if*—the first time it ended was not a down-in-flames, "I never want to see you again!"–style breakup, I have to say it might work. I *like* the idea of an old flame.

(Note: This does not necessarily apply to ex-husbands.)

I do think it's possible to rekindle that old magic . . . if your date gets lit enough.

If Warren Beatty wanted to date me after all this time . . . maybe. But I don't think that's a problem I'll have. I'd also consider dating the boyfriend who I later figured out swung the other way. I know, sounds like a lost cause—but he was a lot of fun, and I wouldn't mind trying my hand at swinging him back.

It's Okay to Be a Parent Who Dates

HIS, MINE, AND OURS

When I head out for groceries—yes, I shop for things besides men—I usually wind up at Bristol Farms, a high-end supermarket in Beverly Hills. This place promotes itself as "an extraordinary food store," but it's also a pretty damn good place to guy-watch.

You've gotta love California: Even the supermarket parking lots are full of characters who could easily push their shopping carts into a three-picture deal. But mixed up with all the lovable loonies are perfectly dateworthy men—you've just got to keep your eyes peeled for bargains . . . the kind you can't get with in-store coupons.

I was on the phone in my SUV when I saw a six-foot-plus dark-haired hot-hot-hottie in ripped jeans and a black T-shirt. He was bent at the waist (nice ass!), trying to reason with a three-year-old girl in a green jumper who was eating little round bubblegum balls out of the box and swallowing them whole.

The Oracle is nothing if not a lifesaver when it comes to small children on the verge of choking to death, panicking their handsome, helpless fathers. Hopping out of my SUV, I sauntered over to them and (remember your Dating 101?) ignored the father as I poured all my attention on his stubborn kid.

"Honey, I'm wearing green today, too," I told the little girl, who looked up at me with an angelic smile as she popped three more gumballs down her throat. She wasn't going to go quietly. I was hoping her father might be the pushover of the family.

"Dude, I know it's none of my business, but maybe she shouldn't swallow the gum," I suggested to him, gazing up at him in a concerned, but not accusatory, way.

"I just don't know what to give her," he fretted aloud. "She loves gum so much and she just won't listen to me."

Lightbulb time. "Honey, I *love* Gummy Bears," I told the little girl. "Maybe we should go in the market and buy some for you!" She nodded and took hold of my head. See? Girls always turn to me for advice.

As I took her hand and led her into the store, I had only one thought going through my mind: "My God—this guy is so hot." (He came with us into the market, in case you were wondering if I'd started a kidnapping racket on the side. I don't recommend breaking the law just to impress a handsome man—smacks of desperation.)

The relief on the father's face was palpable; I'd chewed up and spit out his little gumball crisis. "I just want to thank you . . ." he began.

I cut right to the chase. This was no time to mull over other parenthood concerns. You reach the point where you need the 411 on someone in order to know if you should stay the course or cut and run.

"I only wish you were single because I'd like to go out with you," I said to the father.

"I *am* single," he remarked. "It didn't work out between . . ."

I cut him off. There's a time and place for the exes conversation, and it's not in front of the child. The Big Dog has rules, even if the kid seems too young to grasp the particulars. Children are very perceptive when it comes to their parents—especially when it comes to things like tone of voice. Since you can never really know for sure how much the kid is getting, it's never fair to diss mom or dad in front of them.

They'll hate you if you do it, and they'll hate you if you allow it to be done.

Pressing my card into his palm, I smiled at him and handed him the nearest box of Gummies. "Bye-bye, honey," I said to the cutie.

Then I said goodbye to his daughter.

That night, the father called me for a drinks date the following Friday, when his ex would have their daughter.

It's just that easy.

KID STUFF

As a parent who's single and available and sexual, you have to take precautions. Your children aren't eager to see you with a mate, or even see you on a date. They don't see you that way, and they shouldn't have to if they don't want to.

My kids are totally grossed out when I'm dating someone new. But they're also an amazing focus group, even when they have no clue they're doing it. They have knee-jerk reactions to anyone I bring home. I don't want you to think I have a revolving door—they meet only a select few, the chosen few, on their way to the Mother Country.

One time, my son was telling me to get rid of the boyfriend. Now, this particular boyfriend was young, rich, sexy, and very polite to my kids, so I was reluctant to let that one go. I said, "Give him a chance, Nathan." My son said, "Mom, I can tell you're not sure about him anymore. Get rid of him. You'll hang the collage on the wall and in two months it'll be down." He's right: When I've spent a little time with a new boyfriend, I have a habit of making collages of photos: "Here was the ski trip, the football game, the shopping extravaganza." And then, all of a sudden, they're gone—the boyfriends, that is. The collages have a way of staying on the wall and mocking me.

My son knows me. He's usually right. So his words put a quick kibosh on the too-good-to-be-true heir.

Nip It in the Bud If He's Mr. Nice Guy No More

STALK TALK

A lot of women have to deal with serious, call-the-cops stalkers. These are the lowest of the low—the scumbags who don't take no for an answer. You can't play with them; you have to break things off firmly and turn them in if they don't get the picture.

You want to talk about world-class stalkers, though? Back in my modeling heyday, I was living in a small, red-brick townhouse on the Upper East Side. One night I was hanging out with my friend Iman, who's now married to David Bowie, when this fucking guy who was obsessed with me scaled a wall to get inside my room. He crawled up to dangle this controlled substance in front of the window, as if I was gonna open up for this insane, obsessed sycophant. He was like the vampire scraping on the window in *Salem's Lot*. "Iman, there's somebody at the window," I said. "Who the fuck is that?" she said. "Don't let him in, don't let him in! Call the police." So we did, and that was the end of that.

Guys, it's nice to be wanted. And we know, some of you don't mean any harm when you go to all kinds of lengths to chase us and win our hearts. But when you're at the point of climbing the walls, you can pretty much assume you've climbed too far.

WHEN YOUR DISS GOES AMISS

Speaking of aggressive men, I have a story that reminds me of the importance of knowing when to back down. It fits here. It's a story I hate telling—I still get pissed off thinking about it—but I'll bite the bullet for the greater good.

The second day of my working trip to Cape Town, South Africa, I was invited to show up for an ICE models party that night at the hottest club in the city.

Everything about it sounded fabulous. Every A-list model on the continent would be there—and none of the "America's next top models" we were traveling with. (I don't mean anything by that: The girls on the show were hot, but this party put them on my B list.)

There were so many giraffe-girls in this club that I actually felt short. Looking around, I also realized why so many girls in the United States have a hard time getting work. These women were show-stoppers and they arrived in packs like hyenas.

But enough about other women. Spotlight on Janice, *puhleeze*.

I was sitting on a barstool sipping my mineral water when a man who looked like the African James Gandolfini grabbed the stool next to mine and planted his rather ample ass on it. After a quick glance, I went back to minding my own business—until the goon leaned close to me and laid it right on the line.

"Would you like to go home with me, baby?" he asked in English, but with a thick African accent. Before I could turn him down, he added, "I want you. You're my type."

I raised my perfect Anastasia Beverly Hills–sculpted brow and replied firmly, "No, thank you."

He persisted. "I said I want you in my bed tonight," he demanded.

"Even if you owned all the De Beers diamonds, sweetcake, it's not happening," I replied, turning my back on him. There are some men who need more than a subtle turndown. They need an absolute turn-off to make them go away. And even then it doesn't always work out.

Before I could draw my next breath, he rammed his back into mine and knocked me off my barstool—*hard*. Landing on the floor, I was so winded I couldn't even get up. At this point, I was pretty much hating South Africa.

With tears of embarrassment floating in my eyes, I looked up at this asshole through my running mascara. He was standing over me, laughing.

Rage filled every molecule of my being, but I calmly looked him in the eye and said, "Excuse me—do you have any idea what you just did to me?"

"Oh, fuck you," he said, sneering down at me as I attempted to stand up. No one else extended a hand to help me—which, looking back, should have given me a clue. For a minute, I thought he was going to shove me down *again* because he moved his massive hand in my direction. Instead, he just sneered. "I should have knocked your skinny ass out into the street," he said, raising his hand for effect.

"Big mistake," I said, remembering how Julia Roberts fired back at those Beverly Hills dress-store bitches who refused to help her in *Pretty Woman*. I finally made it to my feet, testing myself to see if I'd slipped any disks when I landed on my tailbone. *Is my tailbone insured?* I was wondering.

"You owe me an apology," I spat. "You hurt me. You really hurt my back."

"An apology?" he said, amused. "If you're waiting for me to apologize, then you're out of your fucking mind."

At that point, he turned his back again.

I shouldn't have done it. In retrospect, I should have stood up and marched out of there; after all, I was in a foreign country—I didn't know *anyone* on this turf. I couldn't even figure out who invited me to this fucking event. I should have called it a night, but for better or for worse, that's not the Big Dog.

What *shouldn't* I have done? I shouldn't have hocked a loogie from the deepest part of my throat, worked it around while standing up, and then spit it directly into the bastard's face. But that's exactly what I did—for worse, I guess.

The asshole didn't even wipe away my spit, which was running down his face. Instead, he just snapped his two fat fingers—and suddenly thirty mammoth security guards were surrounding me and my hairdresser, Duke, who'd run over to help me. My mind was feebly squeaking, "Check, please!" when these no-neck guards picked both of us up like toothpicks, rammed us through the front door (not a fun way to leave a room, especially for a tall woman), and threw us out into the gutter like leftover meat being tossed to stray dogs.

Kicked to the curb in a Third World country. Great ego boost.

What followed was humiliation and hardcore pain. Duke could barely stand up; he was diagnosed with whiplash. My back was still killing me from that first fall off the barstool.

The only thing I wanted was my hotel room. But because I'm a woman with a mind, I needed information.

Staggering up to the semisweet security guard outside the club, I asked, "What is the name of the man who started all this trouble because I wouldn't go home and fuck him? I want to know his name because I'm calling the police."

He shrugged, but by now the club's owner was standing over me. His words were quick and clear. "Miss, the police will do you no good," he said. "That man *owns* the police in this town." Now, I've dated men who owned movie studios and baseball teams, but the *police?* That was a new one.

Turns out, my local Gandolfini was the head of the South African mob. He was Tony Soprano for real—and he wasn't used to a woman, or anyone else, telling him no.

I'd called for the check on this guy, and he'd nearly had me rubbed out.

I feel sorry for all the women in that town who've crossed his path over the years and haven't felt empowered enough to, say, hock a loogie on him. Of course, many of them are probably trapped by poverty, and they're certainly all living in some kind of corrupt mob-controlled state. What's *your* excuse the next time you let a guy bully you into doing anything you don't want to? Sure, I got my tailbone bruised for standing up for myself, but I'd rather deal with that than give up my dignity.

I once read about a woman who stood up in Mexican court to accuse a cop of raping her. He'd hauled her to the station, assaulted her on his desk, then offered her a cigarette after. Her husband even had to pay a bribe for her to be released. Yet, as scared as she was, she pressed charges against the SOB.

Thankfully, my situation didn't escalate to anything like that. But who's to say his thirty guards might not have deposited me into a car instead of onto the street? To this day, that thought still gives me the shivers—and makes me furious. How dare he? I'm an author, a supermodel, an American. I'm a member of the goddam PTA. I don't give a shit who runs the mob in South Africa, he has no right.

My advice: Don't take shit from anyone: date, boyfriend, husband, one-night stand, it doesn't matter. I came out of that South African experience wanting to convince every woman in the world to take a self-defense class. It makes me want to shake women and scream, *If you see violence in the eyes of your man; if you have a funny feeling about his intentions; if he raises a hand to do anything other than stroke your hair—get out of there immediately. We can be hurt.*

The check is already written on every man you meet. Feel free to call for it at any time.

A Date's Great, but a Relationship Rocks

RELATIONSHIPLAND

Perhaps you're wandering into Relationshipland. It's easy to do; after all, the borders aren't well patrolled, and they're mostly unmarked. Remember: Most men are megalomaniacal pigs. And so the only way to protect yourself is to become *your own* megalomaniacal pig. In other words, remind yourself—continually—that *he's* not in control. You have the power, at any time, to call for the check . . . and that's the ultimate form of control.

Make demands on your man. It's the only way to get what you want. Don't sit there, acting all demure, and wait for him to read your mind. If you don't ask, you won't get. If I want to go skiing, I make sure he knows it. I don't drop hints—like walking around in my ski suit. I say, "Take me skiing!" If I'm feeling sick and I want someone to come over and bring me soup, I'll call my guy and say, "Could you bring some soup over?" Men aren't mind-readers. News flash: They're not even *trying* to read our minds. We can't blame them for not knowing what we want. How the hell are they supposed to know all the time? Just give them the answers. You're not an SAT. It's okay to cheat.

If a man who's in even a semirelationship with you suddenly stops calling—*do not* call him. Yes, he might be hooking up with another bitch, but there's nothing you can do about it except call for the check. Of course, that's probably not what you'll *want* to do. If you want to hook up with him again, you'll think a call will start the ball rolling. I repeat: *Do not call.* No matter what! If your hand starts to tremble and it keeps coming to rest on the phone, move it to your knee instead. If you call first during a freeze-out, you've lost all the power. He'll have you *and* the other bitch at his mercy.

By the way, the same goes for e-mails. I hate e-mail, anyway. Can you put in any less effort? A freeze has to be a complete freeze—the Internet hasn't changed *everything*.

RELATIONSHIP CASE STUDY

I. IMPULSE BUY

I met Timothy at a local cell phone dealer, and from the start he made my knees shake. Cute doesn't begin to describe this guy. He looked like a young, (real) blond Justin Timberlake, except with no trace of trailer trash. He was tall and thin, but not skinny. With that chiseled, Norwegian Viking feature thing going, he was beyond adorable.

Timothy helped me look at new camera phones, which was as good as any other way I've met a man.

He's a bit younger than I am. I mean, he's twenty-three. Food for thought. He also explained right away that his family owned a major broadcasting empire. The deal was, he had to work at the store because his megamillionaire grandfather was a little old-school and felt it was important to start at rock bottom. Timothy was putting in his time—which was exactly what I planned to do with him.

"Dude, are you into football?" I asked him, flashing the pearly whites in his direction. It wasn't my fault that I came to the store that day in a miniskirt and transparent Calvin Klein T-shirt.

"What guy isn't into football?" he replied, flashing his equally pearly whites right back at me. With this guy as my salesman, it took all my restraint to restrain myself from ordering PDAs for the entire PTA.

"Well, maybe you want to see my son play football on Friday night," I said, watching to see if he'd freak when I mentioned my son. "But there's a tiny catch."

By now, Timothy was practically putting on his jacket to go. "Yeah, yeah, yeah, what's the catch?"

"Dude, you have to be at my house by noon. The game is far away. Be there," I said, giving him my address and my best leg flash all at the same time.

That Saturday, he pulled up in a spanking new black Land Rover. "What car should we take?" he asked.

I didn't reply. I just slid onto his very soft leather seats and told him he looked truly fabulous in faded jeans and a black T-shirt.

We waited a second until my son and his friend piled into the car. I glanced at Nathan, though, and saw a deep scowl come over his face. Obviously, my boy didn't want me to be out with this boy!

The grimace happened before things got a little hotter. On the way to the game, my younger man decided to rub my back a bit to keep me awake while he was driving. The moment his tender young fingertips touched my back, my son went into how-dare-you-touch-my-mother mode. By the time we left the car Nathan was fuming, which put a bit of a taint on the entire romantic drive (though, come to think of it, all that anger may have helped his game).

"He shows no respect," Nathan whispered to me.

I just sighed. I wanted to grab my cell phone and dial Demi to ask if Rumer had a problem the first time she saw Ashton give her a friendly love pat in the SUV.

For the rest of the day, Nathan played baby bodyguard. All I'd done is get an innocent little back rub, and he just looked at me like I was a hooker!

During halftime, after some discreet hand-holding with Timothy, I left him at the snack stand to find my son.

"Who is this guy? Where did he go to school? What do we know about him?" Nathan demanded. "Do we know his parents? I want to talk to him and find out his intentions."

Was this my son or the father in a Victorian novel?

After a silent, hands-off drive home, I found myself in the midst of a new Cold

War. Days passed without anyone saying a word—until I knocked on my son's door one night and told him the last thing he wanted to hear: "Timothy wants to talk to you on the phone." No response.

The following weekend, we tried it again. Timothy drove us to my daughter Savvy's soccer game, and my son actually spoke to him a little bit. Just when I was feeling a ray of hope, we pulled up in the parking lot and I spotted Soccer Dad! I've had a thing for this guy for the past two years . . . and now, for the first time, he was getting out of his Mercedes. *Alone.* For once, I showed up with a twenty-three-year-old boy and Soccer Dad walked the planks of the stands like they were a runway. Standing only breathing distance from my face, he ignored Timothy and said, "Hey, Janice, I was wondering if you want to go skiing sometime."

Why do some men wait till *after* they think they've missed their big chance to make a move?

I don't do fifty-yard-line dumps, especially when the guy drove me to the game. "I'm sorry, but I can't. This is my boyfriend. He's an Abercrombie & Fitch model."

Timothy smiled warmly, proud to be with me and relieved that I was not going to humiliate him by accepting an offer I was *dying* to accept, and that I spent years making happen. Soccer Dad was a good sport (it figures); he took his loss stoically and moved on.

A few seconds later, Timothy whispered into my ear, "I had no idea what I was in for when I met you. But I like your energy."

Making matters worse, my sweet young boyfriend had a bright idea. "I want you to meet my mother," he suggested sweetly. I was turning down Soccer Dad and being put on a collision course with the Matriarch.

II. HARD FACTS

We weren't exactly sleeping together. We were making out. But he was a Leo, so he was pushing his case. Been there?

What do you do when you just *can't?* (This also works when you don't want to *yet.*)

In this case, I was in the *can't* category. Why? All right, girls, forgive me, but you know how it is: The truth is, I had a hemorrhoid—and one that was more painful than discovering that first gray hair. So I kept hiking up my pants while he kept trying to pull them down. My kids were gone for the evening, but it was like I had my own boys vs. girls wrestling match in my bedroom.

He thought I was being modest. God, that he honestly believed Janice Dickinson is shy is really why I wouldn't sleep with him! If it weren't for the damn hemorrhoid, I'd have been walking around stark naked. I'd show pink in the blink of an eye. But not that night.

Because he's a man, this only made him want me even more. Playing hard to get intensifies the get. Any man who claims he can't tell the difference between "No fucking way, you're raping me!" and "Not now, honey," belongs in court. Tell it to Judge Judy.

Playing hard to get is the best way to get him hard.

III. MEET THE FUCKERS

Meeting your young soon-to-be lover's highly dysfunctional but obscenely wealthy family—especially the two people who screwed not that terribly long ago and brought him onto the planet—is no cakewalk.

But I hadn't seen anything until my little electronics heir pal, Timothy, took me to his family's Malibu beach house on a Sunday morning for the bitch-and-moan family brunch. From the moment I walked through the French doors and stomped off my sandals after a flirty, kissy walk on the beach, I took a look around and made a snap judgment: I sensed that this family was utterly insane on a chemical level. And when I'm right, I'm right.

There was an older uncle checking out my ass and almost panting when we shook hands. Uh-uh: Even I won't climb the family tree in the name of dating a wealthy man.

"Janice, honey," Timothy said, "I'd like you to meet my mother." On the "m" of "mother," there should have been a swell from some invisible orchestra pit. The mother was busty, red-headed, and curvy, very Ann-Margret—emphasis on *Ann* in one of her more recent, creepy roles. I could tell she was exactly my age, even if she couldn't be sure I was her age. And I could tell instantly that the bitch was judgmental. (What? Yeah, I guess she may have had a point.)

Everyone, including the guys, was working on being the coolest fucking bitch in the room. By now, everyone knows my rep: it's like when the quickest draw in the Wild West enters the saloon—all the local gunslingers want to start a gunfight, just to test her out.

Mom got the first word out because I allowed her. After all, as a mother myself, I feel it's only polite to respect the womb that bore the baby loverman. Mom is going to hate you regardless, but show her respect until the hatred is uncaged.

"I don't judge what my children do," said Mommie Nearest, leaning so close to my face that I got a couple of deep breaths of 0 percent oxygen and 100 percent Chanel No. 5. "Honestly, Janice, I think you're great. I think you and my little boy together are just great."

We were all done. So was lunch.

At lunch, I picked up my fork and dug into the shrimp salad. This was no time to let the family spread rumors that I'm anorexic or bulimic. I even ate a careful bite of the sourdough roll, and braced myself as my body went into shock; I don't think I'd ingested white flour since the mid-1990s.

I wasn't nervous. The only person I'd be nervous breaking bad-carb bread with is Osama bin Laden. (Actually, I'd skip the lunch, give him a shave, and teach him how to treat women right.)

Everything at this lunch seemed to go just right—maybe *too* right. The father arrived late in a blue Brooks Brothers suit, shook my hand, and then carefully kissed the top of his wife's head, as if it were the one spot he could stand to put lips on. My new boyfriend wasn't even paying attention; he was more focused on grabbing my knee under the table. Foreplay in front of the family. Are the Kennedys like this?

A few hours later, I fell into that early-relationship haze where you truly believe your future bedmate's parents are the most wonderful people you've ever met in your life. Even in the most special relationships, this is usually a short-lived period. I couldn't stand the perv uncle, who talked about only money, money, and money. He did have a daughter Savvy's age, and for a moment I wondered if they might make good friends—they could bond, read books together. But that was another early haze fantasy—wanting to match all members of your family with members of his family. In reality, I wouldn't want her under his influence—she'd come home reading the *Wall Street Journal* instead of *Harry Potter*.

"We just love everything about you," Mommy Nearest said on my way out. Funny that she chose my exit to say this—that was probably her favorite thing about me. I was only half listening; my mind was still reeling from the uncle's money monologue. Some of it was intriguing, of course; after all, this family owned half of Massachusetts. But then I shook myself out of it; I was for true love, not cash. I took a glance at my new boyfriend; his teeth were so big and white they were like little square clouds.

Strangeness be damned—I wanted into this fucked-up family. I thought we had a future.

We definitely had a now.

Our first night in my bedroom was spent kissing and touching. During a break, Timothy spotted a heart-shaped frame I have on my nightstand. It didn't have a picture in it.

"Who goes in there?" Timothy asked, taking the bait.

"Maybe you," I said.

But then the damned strangeness started creeping up to bite us on our pretty little asses.

I'd worn one of my best Chanel frayed jackets to the parents' home. The following day, Timothy told me, his mother had purchased twenty of the same type of jacket. Imitation is flattering, but when your lover's mom starts trying to imitate you, it's also alarming.

It was becoming obvious to me she was going to remake herself as me and demand that he force me out of his life. She was going to turn my sweet little buddy into a motherfucker, if only in her own off-kilter mind. I could just hear her screaming at him: "She's forty-nine, you're twenty-three—you do the math!" Serious mama's boy syndrome there. Would he cave and break it off with me when the time came? Or would he grow up?

On my side: Supermodel legs. *You* do the math.

Timothy treated me like a queen. He took me to the Four Seasons in Beverly Hills for breakfast, where two people can dine on egg whites, avocado, and cottage cheese on wheat for seventy-five bucks without a tip or valet parking. After a few sips of his fifteen-dollar orange juice, we went back to my house, which is always very quiet, and sometimes—like it was that morning—childless.

After many moons (too many) we finally made love for the first time. He was very sweet about the whole thing; he insisted the age thing meant nothing to him, that he'd never felt more for anyone. He even told me he loved me. Of course, no one said anything about the age thing in that moment; I could only wonder whether it was ongoing, behind-Janice's-back conversation with Mommie Nearest.

I sent him home before my daughter got back from school. I was happy. I was in love.

Then, for three days, he didn't call.

I reminded myself of my own rules: No talking. No e-mailing. No asking the proverbial question: *Was it good for you?* All you can do is pretend that the guy is gone from the earth. You work out. You go about your life. When you want to pick up the phone, you pick up a toothbrush instead.

I've never had better breath.

Timothy eventually resurfaced and invited me on a skiing trip up north for the weekend. He talked about how we'd hit the slopes, but I was hoping we'd be hitting the sheets, too. It was that giddy time early in any relationship where you organize entire shopping trips that cost you a fortune in the name of love. Screw American Express. You can't buy enough new outfits that scream, "I'm seducing someone new!"

I was in the middle of Ski Chalet, a store in Los Angeles, checking out a hot pink down jacket, when Timothy called on my cell.

"What's shakin'?" I said.

"Janice, I'm so sorry, but my family is sending me to Seattle this weekend to explore a new business venture," he blurted out. "We'll have to postpone the skiing trip."

Score one for the family. His mother was doing just what I knew from experience she would do. She was removing me from the picture by sending him out of the picture.

"I'd like to discuss this with you. Stay by your phone and wait for my call," I said calmly before hitting "end call" on him.

I went into the ladies' room and redialed his number. He'd barely said hello when I started screaming into my cell. "Listen, Junior—I just spent three thousand dollars on ski boots. Maybe I'll find someone else to take me skiing. Maybe I'll sit by the fire with some millionaire who appreciates a woman who gets herself ready for a trip. Maybe you'll never hear from me again. So enjoy the sound of my voice for the last time."

In the most pathetic, soft voice, he begged me, "Don't do that."

I said, "I want answers. Why is everyone cock-blocking when the two of us want to be together?"

He said, "This is an opportunity to get into business with my father. I can get a better job with better pay."

I knew I needed to shift gears, or Mommie Nearest would win by TKO. In a more civil tone, I replied, "Why didn't you tell me that from the start? I'm very supportive when it's truly about business."

Four days later, he was standing on my doorstep with a bunch of white calla lilies.

Did he really go out to seek a job opportunity? Or did his mother just want him away from me and recruit his father to help her out?

The jury was out, but I suspected cock-blocking. Call it mother's intuition.

Timothy's family weren't the only ones a bit peeved at the idea of him filling my generation gap. It's clear that my daughter, Savvy, was cautious about this younger man. She's like that with everyone new because she doesn't want to see me hurt. She's at that age where Mom as a real human being grosses her out. If I so much as pull a shoulder strap down to pose for a picture, she'll say, *"Mooooom!"*

It's funny; I'm the one who's supposed to be cautious for her, but she likes to protect me.

When Timothy and I were around her, I was always careful not to touch him or kiss him. You have to protect your children above all things. (Kiss my ass, Omarosa.)

Before a trip to Seattle, Timothy came over "to hang." That's how you can tell if your boyfriend might be too young—he still hangs.

He did something more, which made me want to hang *him*. Timothy took it upon himself to "borrow" my cell. And it's not like he didn't have his own—he just took out this little loan so that he could scan through all of my numbers! When I caught his sorry ass, he was deeply absorbed in investigating the last ten people I called.

When it comes to dating in the electronic age, frankly, I suspect the pioneer women had it easier. If their horses were parked outside someone's barn in the next town, it was clear they were fucking the farmer. But their hog-butcher husbands had to search the entire countryside for such liaisons, which must have been pretty exhausting. He couldn't just go inside their log cabin and snoop around in her wood-burning PC.

My boyfriend's desperate sleuthing worked my last nerve.

"Hey, James Bond," I said to him. He jumped a mile and gave me a shit-eating grin. "You're caught. Drop it. Back away from the phone."

He dropped it like it was a hot coal.

"How would you feel if I went over to your house at three in the morning without asking and found you were in bed with some other broad?" I asked him. His eyes went wide. "You wouldn't like that spy mission, and I don't appreciate your little undercover work. Who am I, North Korea?"

He gulped.

"My cell phone is off limits to you. Why? Because you'll find numbers there that you don't want to see," I said as a warning. Janice Strategy number 14: Take a bad situation and use it to your own advantage—flip it. Sometimes, a young boyfriend still needs schooling.

"Like *whose* number?" he demanded, like he was going to take the upper hand. Right.

"The Cs begin with Clinton and include Clooney," I responded flatly. Was it true? Does it matter? He gulped, again, and swore he'd use his own phone from now on.

The lesson here, for men and women alike: Seek and ye shall find—something you don't want to find. If you feel you *must* look . . . call for the check.

IV. THANKFULLY IT'S OVER

I was sick as a dog with a sinus infection when Timothy called with an amazing offer. "I'd like to fly you and Savvy up to my parents' house in Palm Springs for a family Thanksgiving," he cooed. "Everyone is dying to see you again and meet Savvy."

I felt so bad I was sure Reuters was already spell-checking my obituary, but this offer was too good to be true. Armed with two weeks' supply of the strongest antibiotics and the shortest black skirts, I packed up and convinced my daughter that this would be fun. She wasn't so sure, but she agreed reluctantly to go along for the adventure. Sometimes I think I might get further trusting *her* gut feelings rather than my own.

We arrived on Thanksgiving Day, when I swear my fever had spiked to 104 degrees. I felt like one of those steer skulls you see by the side of the road in the desert.

From the start, everyone loved Savvy. They spent the day talking to her (very friendly), hanging with her (very nice), and even watching movies with her (a sweet touch). When I could muster up the strength, I macked with Timothy in the hidden chambers of their thirty-room third house—a mansion no one ever used, though it was kept *Architectural Digest* ready at all times. You could take a dump in the middle of the floor and turn your back and it would disappear.

As I hungrily devoured my host, I was dreading the meal. This was no supermodel thing: By this time, I'd taken so many antibiotics my stomach was doing heaving somersaults. I was dizzy with fever. The thought of scarfing down a huge meal is alien to me anyway. Supermodels don't overeat and then sit around on the sofa with their belts undone.

Around 4:00 P.M., everyone was summoned into the dining room for a spread of food that could have fed every *Cosmo* cover girl from 1975 to the present day.

The minute I smelled turkey, I got that queasy feeling I had when I was pregnant. (Don't worry, I wasn't. Thank God!) But I knew I was going to have to work Thanksgiving like a runway. So I worked it.

I sat down gracefully and said the prayer demurely. I kept things down when the maid put a heaping pile of stuffing on my plate. I even tried to shove a few bites down my throat. I was doing great.

That's when my body decided we were going to do a scene from *The Exorcist*. I searched my brain for ways to projectile vomit tastefully, and found none.

"If you all will excuse me," I said regally, standing up and sauntering out of the room, then running for the nearest john as soon as I was out of sight. On my way out, I overheard the uncle whisper gleefully, "I told you—they're all bulimic!"

In this precious little Laura Ashley bathroom, I rid myself of the Thanksgiving stuffing, and everything else I'd eaten in 2004. The upside was, I'd never seen my stomach flatter! But the downside was horrifying: I clogged the toilet. One flush, and I'd be sending a river of puke running down the halls.

What could I do? I cleaned up, then left the bathroom, without a word to anyone about the mess I'd left.

I returned to dinner, where everyone but Savvy thought I was a tragic bulimic.

The next day began with Timothy kissing me sweetly and offering me a cup of tea. I sipped and smiled, feeling a little better. At breakfast, I noticed we were the only ones around the table, which made it easier to ask for dry toast without furthering my rep as a walking eating disorder.

The very wealthy uncle, who made his millions selling McMansions, was visiting, bragging nonstop about his bank account and how much he loved spending money. At one point he asked Savvy if she wanted a horse. Savvy wasn't impressed with him as a person, but she's no fool—she nodded and smiled. It's okay, she knew he was full of shit. She's my daughter, after all. When I walked by the uncle in the hallway, he grabbed my ass. He's lucky I didn't ram that big bank account of his right up *his* ass.

I mean, there is a time and place for ass grabbing, but it's not on Thanksgiving weekend with my boyfriend and daughter a room away.

Later that night, the rich uncle dropped his pants in his room, with the door wide open, as I was walking past. I saw him, just as he'd wanted. But so did Mommie Nearest. I thought she'd flip out. Instead, she ignored it. I guess saying anything would have been admitting that her family was fucked up already without me. Everyone thinks they'll be the first normal rich person, but nobody ever is.

That day, Timothy took me to his parents' favorite chichi golf club in the next town, where I ran into a model friend of mine who married a multimillionaire thanks to . . . *moi!*

How did it happen? One night, her man had told me that he wanted to propose to her right away, but he didn't have a ring handy. Never one to stop the momentum of a proposal (second thoughts are a dangerous thing), I gave him my mother's ring.

"Janice, what should I do if she says yes?" he asked.

"You marry her!" I said. Sometimes men go a little brain dead.

A few days later, he returned my mother's ring and gave her a ten-carat diamond. A month later, they were married in Aspen. His best wedding gift to her: no prenup. A month after they were married, his stock shot up and he became a billionaire. So when I saw her again, she was a billionairess.

Which brings me back to me.

Did I ever get a thank-you note for my role in bringing these two lovebirds together? Or a Prada throw? Or some stock options? No, I did not. And I'm the one who stayed with her for the entire too-ill-to-move weekend after she got her breasts done. In fact, I sent her to my doctor and told her which breasts to buy. A week later, she met the man of her dreams.

I did everything for her but marry the guy myself.

Fast-forward to that Thanksgiving weekend, when I ran into my girlfriend. She and her billionaire hubby had a house next door to Timothy's family. I saw her on the golf course and we hugged warmly.

Neither of us was playing golf. We were just tagging along with our guys.

"Don't you want to play?" Timothy asked me.

"My breasts are too big," I complained. "They get in the way of golf." I adopted a mock golf pose with my boobs all scrunched up and my ass sticking out provocatively.

"Stick with them," my girlfriend told me. "They're so loaded it's ridiculous."

V. GOING FOR BROKE

After a quiet family breakfast the next morning, we left for the airport. Mommie Nearest said to Timothy, "Honey, you should be watching your money." She knew he'd flown me to her house for the whopping cost of $105 round-trip. Savvy's ticket was half price. I pulled a few dollars out of my purse and handed it to Timothy right in front of her.

"For gas money," I said. "Let's drive back."

Mommie Nearest interjected, "Oh, good, you're *driving* to Los Angeles. I'll go with you!"

Fuck!

She sat in the back seat the entire time, chattering nonstop. I was quiet in the front seat next to her son. Strange thoughts crowded my mind: *What would she do if he ever proposed to me? She'd do anything in her power to ruin any wedding.*

Which means we'd have to elope. No *InStyle*, but you can't have everything.

I have news for everyone. The Big Dog won't be satisfied without everything. And you shouldn't be either.

VI. THE PAIN OF STRAIN

I spent an entire day in December with Timothy doing all of his Christmas shopping. I was out all fucking day finding stuff for his friends and family. I spent the whole day giving, giving, giving. Sure, it was his cash, but still—it's the thought that counts.

After all this, he comes back to my home with me and casually informs me that he's heading back to his place to chill out with a beer.

Hello! I spent the entire day in his service as Mrs. Claus. Now he was begging for Mrs. Claws.

I was really hurt. I gripped my heart like the star of some black-and-white melodrama. "There's the door," I said icily. "Hit that fucker hard."

"What?" He was bewildered.

"It's time for you to leave," I said.

"I want to say goodbye to your daughter."

Coming to my aid, Savvy asked, "Why aren't you staying over again?"

He mumbled again something about needing to chill. Which will be easy because I'm going to give him Siberia.

He came downstairs and I escorted him to the door and pressed the garage door opener. I said, "Enjoy Miller time. Because Janice time is over."

He said, "I don't understand why you all of a sudden changed."

"I all of a sudden raised the bar."

Walking back in the house, I slammed the door and got upset. I helped him—you might think he'd want to draw me a bath and make love to me. But no, he wants to go nurse a beer. He deserved to get the check.

I called my best friend and cried. When Timothy called later, I wasn't picking up the phone. Don't give an inch when you're right by a mile.

True to her name, Savvy knew something was wrong. She came downstairs and caught me crying and said, "What's wrong, Mom?" She gave me a hug and said, "Men are idiots." And she didn't even need to read my books to figure this out. Children of single parents are always concerned when they see their parents with a new person who has clearly broken their heart.

When Savvy was out, I started slamming doors and flicking light switches. Off and on, knocking things over like Bobby Brown. I was in full drama-queen mode—Ava Gardner with a side of Lana Turner.

I was fucking miserable—for myself and for the entire female gender. This is how it is in dating, my friends. The way it was and always will be.

I started making those resolutions we all make at one time or another: I will never give my heart to another man. I'm through with men.

The next day, Timothy came over with two dozen red roses and a sheepish grin.

It was back on.

Don't Do Anyone You Might Regret

YOUR BEST FRIEND'S BOYFRIEND (IF YOU GO FOR IT, I'LL BREAK YOUR KNEECAPS)

There are certain unbreakable rules in life and this is one of them: Stay the fuck away from your best friend's boyfriend. You never should have anything to do with your girlfriend's boyfriend. Never, ever, ever, ever.

Many years ago, I had a big crush on Jon Peters, but I never took it to first base because I was friends with his soon-to-be-wife Christine, and she had the claim on him. Of course, that didn't mean my feelings just went away. Each and every time I ran into them, I did a reality check and the crush was still there. But I didn't do that bitch thing that women do to each other. The Oracle didn't flirt, slip a spaghetti strap down, or bat the false eyelashes at him. I didn't engage him in a debate about what constituted a great blow job. That's girlfriend and wife territory. You must put on the brakes and say to yourself, "No matter what . . . I'm not going there."

Even if he hits on you, don't go for it. It's bad for your karma. Instead, make it clear you'll rat him out.

Even if he pulls down his pants in front of you, walk away. Get a good look, but walk away.

I don't have that many absolute rules, but this one is set in platinum.

Maybe you're thinking, "But Janice, I think I'm in love with my girlfriend's boyfriend and I can't take another breath without making a move on this guy."

Bullshit. Go to the gym. Get over it. Take up a hobby. Learn a new language. And please, keep your thong on.

Making a move (or accepting one) from said boyfriend is the lowest of the low. It will only come to crushing blows between all the parties and set you up for mind-boggling, debilitating, can't-even-breathe pain.

I know from experience because I've had girlfriends who have gone after my men. I didn't only take it out on the man. Once, when a friend screwed this guy I liked, I called her to inform her that we would never have anything to do with each other again. I kept my word. *You know who you are, bitch.*

IF HE SAID "I DO," YOU DON'T!

Every single woman has been faced with one of the most painful experiences in life. It's called falling in love with a married man—or, as I like to call it, getting caught up in entanglements you can't untangle.

Don't kid yourself when he whines to you that the wife is a cold bitch who hasn't put out in years. That kind of thing is mostly bullshit of the highest order. He's probably still slipping it to his wife while lying to you, which makes him an LD in my book—a Low Dog. Your dog is also probably getting massages with "happy endings." Married men who cheat are constantly cheating. If a married man cheats once, he'll cheat a hundred times, given the opportunity.

I once got involved with a married guy who told me his wife had grown too fat to enjoy sex anymore. One day I found myself snooping through his car, and I found pictures of his wife. She was dancing at some club—looking beautiful, damn it. And not fat. When he caught me, he saw the photos . . . and I could see the love in his eyes.

There's another classic line men will try if you give them half a chance: "I'd love to leave my wife, but it would break my children's hearts." Was he thinking about breaking little junior's heart when his hand slipped down around your ass?

Married men have plenty of excuses and justifications for their behavior and their feelings, but what about your feelings? Ask the cocksucker *that!* Try it: *What about* moi? He'll look at you like you're speaking another language, and I don't mean French.

Every "other woman" clings to the promise that her two-timing man will leave his wife and hook up with her for good. It's just a big pipe dream, even when he doesn't have have a big pipe. Chances are, he'll never dump his wife. He hasn't dumped her yet, whether it's because he likes the social status of having a wife, or because he doesn't want to split up his cash in a messy divorce, or (yes) because he loves her. For most cheating married men, the thought of giving the wife half in a divorce is a nonstarter. If you're a wife who's dreaming otherwise, give it up: He'll dump you before he writes that check. A man has to be filthy rich to not care about half of his net worth—and when he's that rich, he cares about it even more.

Believe me, I've been there.

If you just can't say no to dating a married man, at least you should dignify yourself by assuming the proper title. You're the mistress. Your services are simple: You fuck the guy and then he goes home to his wife. You're basically like one of those amazingly lifelike rubber vaginas you find in a sex-toy store. I'm sorry, but does it really do you any good to sugarcoat it?

Believe me, I feel your pain. It's torture to fall in love with a married man, but there's only one solution. You must walk away. If you want to mess with him as you walk away, hire a male model from an agency and "run into" your married lover. It's a little bit of payback and that's always fun . . . but he still ain't leaving his wife.

When it comes to married men who are getting their daily rocks off with you while taking their wives to nightly social functions, the most important thing to remember is that *you have the power*. It's never too soon to call for the check on a married man. He will fuck you with total abandon and worship you for a while, but when it ends—and end it will—it's going to hurt. A lot. My last go-round with a married man resulted in loss of sleep and weight (well, it wasn't all bad, I guess), not to mention the guilt.

Please check his finger for a ring, then "Check, please!" him if the finger isn't naked.

SEPARATION ANXIETY

There is a breed of man out there who seems datable because he is separated from his wife. "Oh, joy!" we're supposed to think to ourselves, "This amazing catch is back on the market! I almost missed my chance!"

You might be fooled into thinking "separated" means "heading for a divorce," but think again. To some pigs out there, it just means "taking a break from marriage." Separated men think of separation as a sex vacation. They're going back home eventually, but they want to give their dicks a nice holiday in the meantime.

For many women, this kind of guy is hard to understand. One of the biggest mysteries of life is, "How separated is he?" How do you know if he has really broken ties with the little woman?

Clue 1: As the new girlfriend, you should be able to call him any time you want. If he has a problem with that, it means he's still more married than separated.

Many men will shy away from such frequent phone contact, insisting, "I just don't like to talk on the phone, baby."

You counter and say, "I can't sleep without hearing your voice."

Clue 2: If your new man is busy all weekend, every weekend, I've got news for you: He's spending that time with his wife and kids. He's too busy for you and you need to move on.

Men who aren't married have free time on the weekends. It's just that simple. The same goes for holidays. It's great if he's seeing his children, but not if he's spending too much time with the supposed ex. It's important for him to act like a father, but not like a husband. Just because Santa traditionally brings the presents overnight doesn't mean Daddy has to pull a sleepover on Christmas.

And if your separated man is still living at home for supposed financial reasons, tell him this one's on you and call for the check.

WHAT HAPPENS WHEN THE INK ON HIS DIVORCE PAPERS IS STILL DRYING

This is how you date *really* recently divorced men—and I don't care if they were married six months or twenty-five years. You *congratulate* them. It shocks them.

Why? Because what most of these guys want is *pity*—and many women will let them cry a river on one shoulder, while they offer a violin serenade on the other. They want you to say, "Oh, I'm so sorry. It must be so hard for you." Instead, say congrats, and move on with your date.

Like I've said, on a date you should be discussing the topics of the day—not the exes, the lawyers, the custody, the who got what. It's boring, unromantic stuff, not date material. If the guy can't discuss anything but those things, call for the check. He's not ready to date and he doesn't deserve you as a mate.

Go with the Flow

BING THERE

The Oracle went on a few dates with millionaire producer Steve Bing. I got him before Liz Hurley got him, and way before Nicole Kidman allowed photo ops of him holding her hand. I hear he's mellowed a lot now, but I had him in the good old days when he was Bing the Merciless. His date of choice: Taking his babe *du jour* to a strip club.

Wearing my cultural anthropologist hat (and heels), I visited a few strip clubs with Bing and his rich friends. I wanted to find out what the boys think while these girls gyrate their asses in front of them. Honestly, I wasn't too impressed; I've seen models reveal just as much skin on much more beautiful sets. In one of these clubs I ran into an old friend of mine—a popular newsman—and watched him peel off a few hundred-dollar bills from a huge roll. I was so excited when he stuffed a C-note into my hand that I stuffed it in my own G-string.

Later, I went to the john and the bill fell in the toilet, where it practically dissolved in the gray water. This rich news dude was actually giving these poor strippers fake hundreds! Even the nice ones aren't that nice!

Cut to Bing, who is a hot guy *and* a rich one—a hard combo to resist. Bing didn't need to give away fake hundreds: He was packing the real deal, and he tossed those bills at the girls without thinking twice. He motioned the prettier girls over to stuff hundreds directly down their bras, which had sad little tassels around the nipples.

But it didn't work out between the Oracle and Bing. I got tired of his type of nightlife. Taking your hot girlfriend to a strip club is like going to a museum when you've got the *Mona Lisa* at home.

And then there was that whole messy business between Bing and Liz Hurley over their son. For the record, Bing makes it perfectly clear when you're dating him that he's not the settle-down type, *at all*—no ifs, ands, or buts. He's not the guy you're going to find in your den flipping channels to see what's on cable. I knew what I was getting myself into with Bing—basically, some great dinners and a few trips to strip clubs.

The Oracle understands a multimillionaire with this mentality. You have to listen to his rules and try not to pin matrimony and fatherhood on the type of man who tells you up front that it's not gonna happen. If men have to respect your rules, you should respect theirs.

If you're the settle-down type, and the guy you're dating is more into settling down for a lap dance somewhere, call for the check.

Don't Move (In) Too Fast

SPEEDING CAN BE HAZARDOUS TO YOUR HEALTH

After my boyfriend Tommy and I met on the set of *The Surreal Life*, he moved in right away—*on the first date*. It was the strangest thing ever: At first it was so romantic, but soon I realized we'd taken that step way too early. I didn't wanna be alone, but it was a big mistake. Take it from me: Don't move too fast. If you rush a new relationship, you might ruin any chances you have for something more lasting, and you can't call for the check as easily if the guy is your roommate.

When your breakfast hits the white noise of your Tylenol P.M. and you look across the table and see the person you're stressing over sitting there in his boxers and a T-shirt he slept in, it complicates life.

Two months later, Tommy was on the way out. I blame it on rooming with Omarosa. I needed to clear the palate.

If You Want to Get Married, Get a Move On

HOW TO MAKE HIM POP THE QUESTION

Let's say you've been dating for about a year (or sixteen days if you're Katie Holmes) and there's been talk of marriage, but no proposal. I have a simple solution: *You* propose.

I was on *The Surreal Life*, and I met a dude named Carey Hart. His rocker-chick girlfriend, Pink, proposed to him when she couldn't wait any longer, and I think that's great. Why wait?

But here's one tip: Do it after oral sex.

Come on, girls—it's all about timing. Is there a better time to rope your man in than after you've just helped him achieve a triple orgasm? If he can't say yes at that moment, he never will. Of course, it doesn't make for the most charming story to tell the family ("Actually, he popped just before I did!"), but it works.

First, you must rise, sit down at the edge of the bed and say, "After careful consideration, I realize that you're the one for me. I love you. I still want you for crazy sex, but before we get back to that, will you marry me?" If you have the cash, you can buy yourself a ring and have him give it to you as a "temp" before he goes out and buys the real thing.

I do think Britney Spears had the right idea when she bought herself that diamond stunner as her engagement ring to Kevin Priceline—I mean, Federline. She got exactly what she wanted—the man and the choice jewelry. Brit also knew that the tabloids wouldn't exactly love her choice in men, but at least the ring was impeccable.

One word about rings.

Several years ago, I was given a skating rink-sized, twenty-three-fucking-carat ring (fuck you, J-Lo . . . fuck you, Paris), and with it came a formal marriage proposal. It was the ring of my dreams, but the sex was the worst in my life. On those cold nights in bed I'd look at that ring and realize I had married for money, and that wasn't a good feeling. You can date for money, but marrying for it is a bad idea.

Later, that ring came in handy. I hocked it, and lived lavishly on it for a year. My divorce was the best part of that whole marriage. No, the ring was.

But if you're in love, it's time to do something about it. I believe that strong women everywhere have to take the ring and proposal into their own hands in this way. Your man will either crumble or give you a slew of excuses that mean you shouldn't keep wringing your hands. He probably will never marry you. Deal with it. One way or the other.

Or he'll say, "Yes . . . oh . . . yes!" What do you do then? You marry him, of course.

I'd call for the check on any man who failed to say yes to your proposal—immediately and enthusiastically.

PART III

Mating

What's Next?

Now that you know everything you need to know (not everything there *is* to know—just the essentials) about having a satisfying, perfect date, you may be wondering how to make sure the guy will call you up for a second date.

Well, a girlfriend of mine once said she sees nothing wrong with oral sex.

Sex . . . It's Even Better Than Sex

THE DIFFERENCE BETWEEN HAVING SEX AND MAKING LOVE

There is no difference.

I repeat: There is no difference between having sex and making love. Someone came up with that idea just to confuse people. Maybe someone with an agenda decided that you should only make love when you're in love, and anything else was just down-and-dirty sex. If you don't have down-and-dirty sex with the love of your life, he'll find someone else to do it with. And so will you, eventually.

Let's say you're in love. You want to drive your loved one crazy with sex. You make him want you to the point where you have sex and make love at the same time. On the other hand, let's say you're not in love. You can still make love to this person, or just jump his bones and pretend it's love. Don't delude yourself. It's all the same parts mixing it up, whether you're with someone who makes your heart flutter or just someone you were curious to see naked.

Women always want to hear their men say, "Let's make love." It's a nice sentiment, girls—I love to hear it, too—but don't believe the hype.

They may be making love to you, but they're also doing you and fucking you at the same time—that is, if they're doing it right.

Just remember that there are two kinds of men—the kind who don't stop when you moan "Don't stop!" and the kind who stop.

A woman needs to be able to get out of the romance-novel mode and say, "Let's go have some hot sex." Believe me, your man may be the love of your life, but he'll be naked before you finish the sentence.

You know how people say, "It's all good"? They're talking about making love and having sex.

THE BEST SEX I EVER HAD—BAR NONE

I knew a guy—I'll call him Carnegie (you'll see why). I met him at the gym at the Parker Meridien Hotel. He asked me if I liked music and I said, "Of *course*," so he invited me to . . . Carnegie Hall. When I met him there, he was wearing a fireman's T-shirt. *Whoa,* I thought. *What's this? Firemen are hot, but a T-shirt for a date at Carnegie Hall? I work in* fashion, *remember?* I didn't quite understand it, but I stopped worrying about it once he got me admitted for free. I didn't see anything to indicate he worked there, but soon he was leading me to this beautiful box to hear David Byrne from the Talking Heads.

Then, as I was sitting in the box, he comes back wearing an Armani suit.

Now I'm completely confused. What's going on? *When in doubt,* I thought, *just roll with it.* Finally, I figured it out: He was a lighting tech at Carnegie Hall.

The one guy who knew how to turn me on was a light flicker.

After about fifteen minutes, he leaned in, and I leaned right in with him, like, *Yeah, this is cool, we're the cutesy couple.* We put our arms around each other.

Then he asked, "Are you single?"

I was like, "Psh—yeah . . . !"

That should have been my warning sign right there. Ladies, I should have been hearing the bells, whistles, and fucking foghorns at that moment. Was I *single?* Never mind—we'll get to that later.

After the concert, he took me downstairs where all the props were, pulled my pants down, and started giving me head right there on the stairs. I was thinking, "Whoa, this guy's for me!" If oral sex didn't already exist, I would have had to invent it. Then another thought crossed my mind: "I can't do this—I'll get arrested. You can't have sex in Carnegie Hall!" I'd always considered Carnegie Hall close to home, ever since I lived there with Mike Reinhardt. I was loving what this guy was doing, but I said, "No, no, no, no, no." I didn't grab him or anything, but I got out of there as quick as I could.

"Call me tomorrow," he said. "We'll have coffee." *Okay, that's cool,* I thought. I was alone, I was in New York, I didn't know anybody. What's the harm?

So the next day I walked by Carnegie Hall and there he was again, right there in the same place. He escorted me in, took me up to the same booth, and banged me like there's no tomorrow. Forget Liam Neeson. This was one guy with a porn-star endowment.

I was trying not to make any noise, because people were working downstairs in the building, and you could hear a pin drop. But I'm the most primate fuck on earth. The noises I make are just insane. Lady Princess wanted to grunt and groan; I just wanted to throw my panties to the ceiling and hope they stuck. But this was Carnegie Hall, so they weren't gonna make it that far. He kept his hand over my mouth and banged me so hard I got rug burns. But it was worth it!

So I started an intense, reckless affair with this guy—we were getting it on in doorways, under pool tables. If there was a flat surface big enough to lean on, we were there holding it up, or knocking it over.

One time, after we were together, I turned to him, all perky, and asked, "So, what are you doing this weekend?"

"I'm going to my brother-in-law's," he said.

I gave him the "is-that-your-sister's-husband?" look and he said, "I'm really sorry. I'm married."

"Married? Are you out of your fuckin' mind?" I didn't approve. Here I was writing a book called *Check, Please!*, and Ms. Know It All had tears welling up in her head and rolling hot off her cheeks. I'd turned away, my hand on the doorknob, so he didn't know how upset I was. *Do I just walk out and not ever see this fool again*, I wondered, *because that's the right thing to do? Or do I give in for the sex?*

"Tell me one thing," I asked. "Why did you lie to me?"

You'll love his rationalization. "Because she's . . . *old*," he sputtered.

"That's not good enough," I sniffled.

"She's fat," he said.

"Well, *that* I understand." Karma will kill you every time.

We kept seeing each other—and I got myself in trouble, because I did the one thing that you're never supposed to do: I fell in love with a married man. It wasn't just sex anymore, even though the sex was an expression of the intensity. It was just horrible what this guy was doing, this society's outcast. (But he was also doing *me*, so . . .)

Why should I care? I wasn't the person he was cheating on. Whose wife is it, anyway?

So we did this for about three to four months. My heart just got broken. How do you get out of it? This guy's wife even found out. She threw him out of the house. He ended up living in the storage room where he banged me. It was very *Hunchback of Notre Dame*.

But still it didn't fizzle out. I'm not kidding you. It doesn't make me look very selective, but I told you at the beginning of this book that I'm imperfect. And I was addicted. He made a couple of trips to see me, I made a couple of trips to see him—it was *on*.

Ultimately, he ended it—with a phone call that absolutely broke my heart. The best sex I ever had led to the worst dumping, bar none. He went back to his wife. He wasn't going to get a job in L.A., and I certainly wasn't going to move to New York and live in a storage room. Worse, he kept calling to see how I was doing. After a raucous Howard Stern appearance I made, he called to say, "I heard you on Howard. You were really brave and good." He was calling me at "our" hotel, and I was in the same room where we'd had all our orgies, so I interrupted his bullshit praise and said, "I just want you to know, I'm in our old room."

"Yeah?" he said smoothly. "I heard you tell Howard you have a boyfriend. Does he make you wet behind the knees?" That's the only way I know if I'm having a good time in the sack, is if I start sweating there—then I know it's on. Now he had me completely obsessing again.

But I laughed it off. I said goodbye, and I did *not* call him back.

Good sex is great and great sex is phenomenal, but a married man is a dealbreaker. And a heartbreaker.

Men Are Not Fuck Machines, Unfortunately

WILL YOU EVEN *GET* NAKED?

If you want to get laid, do not let him eat dessert. It's a basic rule: If he's over forty and he has a drink at dinner and dessert, then nine times out of ten he won't have the stamina for intercourse later. Instead, he'll pass out on you—possibly right on top of you.

Even younger guys can't be totally trusted. Men put in long hours at the office or on the set, and if you feed them booze and carbs and sugar they'll be sleeping by midnight. Cake is your enemy. Alcohol is the devil.

If you do want to get laid, try insisting that you both drink mineral water because you're trying to cut down on drinking. If he wants dessert, tell him it's waiting at home.

If you get home and he'd rather devour Sara Lee than you, give him some cake and withhold the pie—he just called for his own check.

On the other hand, if you're on a date and you definitely *don't* want to get laid, then bring on the Merlot and don't forget that extra-large Death by Chocolate special. There are times when dessert is a girl's best friend. And you can't be arrested for inducing a carb coma.

When a man does fall asleep on you before sex and you're frustrated, it's fine to lay down the law. Just tell him, "If you want to date me, next time take a beauty nap in the afternoon." It'll wound his pride and get his attention fast. If he knows what's good for him, he'll cut out the desserts and step up his game.

Lesson 34

Size Matters

THE LONG AND SHORT OF IT

Over the ages, women have been dogged by the most perplexing dating questions:

Why don't men call?

Why don't men call *back?*

And finally . . . why do itty-bitty, short-guy rock stars think they deserve to date Amazonian supermodels?

Look at the Duran Duran boys—each of them nabbed himself a supermodel who towered above him except during photo shoots, when the girls spent most of their time leaning over the guys' crotches for effect. I've also noticed that Elaine Erwin looks like she's on stilts when she's next to her Indiana rocker husband, John Mellencamp. Of course, the answer to this puzzle is easy: Rockers are sexy, and they consider supermodels the ultimate reward for a job well done.

I recall when John Oates of Hall & Oates hit on me. There he stood, way down below me, staring up at Mount Dickinson.

Frankly, I thought he was semi-adorable, I knew he was rich, and I figured he could certainly introduce me to far taller rockers (if there are any). But I still said no.

What can I say? I'm a man-eater.

BRAIN POWER

Size-wise, a big, fat brain can be a major turn-on.

A big brain is the one physical asset that can overcome a small package. It's great when they're both large and in charge, but that's a rare combo. I don't always need matinee-idol looks on a man to hold my interest, though, especially if he's sharp.

I can't mention his name, but there's a guy who used to run Hollywood—he bought and sold a studio. What the fuck, I'll tell you: His name is Harry Sloan. He was an attorney who used to run the studios, and then he wound up having his own film company; after he bought and sold that, he bought and sold Marvel Comics. Then he bought and sold another company in Europe; he owned television stations in Sweden and Prague; he had his own aviation company. Get the picture? This guy was the jackpot.

I dated him for about four months and then he dumped me. *Damn,* I thought, *the big one got away!* But it wasn't just about the bucks—the truth is, I really liked the guy. He wasn't the most attractive guy, but he had magnetism.

We'd met on a blind date. He took me to the Bel-Air Bar at the Bel-Air Hotel, where we talked for three hours; all of a sudden we just started making out, I was so attracted to him. I know you probably think it's common for me to find myself frenching guys in public, but it's not—I just happen to be writing about every instance in this book, so you're getting a distorted view of things.

What made me want to make out with this guy, who looked very corporate and dry? The fact that he was so bright. The brain and spirit morphed into something more than looks.

This, my friends, is what explains that great unexplained phenomenon: beauty and the geek. Why would a beautiful woman (Julia Roberts) date a strange-looking nerd (Lyle Lovett) or a hot-looking guy make time with a troll? It's chemical. It's pheromones. And most of all, it's this insane need to do it with someone whose brain is so dazzling that you feel you must reward them.

SIZING UP THE COMPETITION

If you believe size doesn't matter, you'll also believe that ugly is the new pretty, it's wrong to be turned off by male breasts, and white's totally fine after Labor Day.

Does size matter? Absolutely. Have you ever been totally indifferent when you saw a guy's unit for the first time? For better or for worse, what he's packing matters, and it matters big-time.

Of course, not everyone wants the same thing. Some like 'em big, some like 'em medium, some like 'em small.

How can you tell if a guy is big without seeing him in a Speedo? Check out the nose, ladies. Not the feet. The nose. Big schnozz, big schlong.

Personality is important. An unsatisfying personality can be a dealbreaker—sometimes even more than an unsatisfying dick.

John Cusack, whom I dated for a while, should have given that some thought. I just read an interview with John where he said that how you can tell you have no connection with a lover is when you realize that she isn't laughing at your jokes. Wrong. You know why she's not laughing at your jokes, John? You're not funny!

If John knew what was good for him, he'd just take his dates to dinner and then take his clothes off—because he's built like a stallion. Sure, he's debonair, and he can act. But you need more than that, honey.

So let's say size matters, but it can never be the only dealmaker. Not beyond a few hot dates.

IS THREE A CROWD?

Speaking of size, the size of your party when you're having sex should be two—unless you're in the mood for an all-out orgy.

There's a phenomenon in Los Angeles that is redefining the classical way we look at "threesomes." Single, eligible, sexy, wealthy men say they want to date me. But they also have a little twit girl (usually in her twenties) lurking somewhere on the side.

Forget the men for a moment and let's focus on the women. These girls are usually broke, completely helpless, very dependent, exceedingly beautiful, and good at putting on an oh-so-innocent, I-just-need-help-from-a-man look. Many of them are aspiring actors and models. These girls will insist that your future boyfriend is nothing more than just an older, richer mentor who is "helping them out." They just don't finish the sentence, which is "of their clothes."

It's total bullshit—because these women will have their legs spread wide the minute you turn your back.

Word of warning: These girls aren't innocent at all, so it's hard to get rid of them. But we must send them back where they came from, or to the Midwest at least. I have nothing against the heartland, but these girls belong in malls working the register at the Gap or Auntie Anne's Pretzels instead of cock-blocking Aunt Janice. They shouldn't be dating choice men—they belong in a storage room up against a wall, which is where many of these girls actually learned their craft anyway.

We need to block the CBs.

My recent run-in with a CB was thanks to my infatuation with Steve, a ruggedly attractive Italian I noticed running on the treadmill next to me at the gym. It didn't take long for me to notice Steve; with his ringlets of blond hair, he looked like he'd just filmed a surfer movie on the way to the gym—something that's actually possible in L.A. After a few not-so-shy glances at his developed pecs and thigh muscles, Steve noticed and introduced himself. He immediately told me he was a film director.

Suddenly, it became clear to me. I'd made out with this guy years earlier at a club, but then it turned out he had a girlfriend, and I never heard from him again.

Now here he was with sweat dripping down his brow, pretending we'd never met. If he hadn't been so gorgeous I might have been insulted. But it was a new day, and why dwell on the past? After an interesting conversation about film, Steve asked if I wanted to come over and watch one of the five hundred movies in his collection.

"We can watch in my screening room," he said with a sexy, knee-buckling smile.

"I'll bring the popcorn," I practically panted.

"Bring enough for three," he replied. I said a silent prayer that the third party was a dog who liked greasy snack food, but no such luck.

"I have a young girl named Maya living with me. She's a student from Germany who wants to become an actress. She's like an intern to me. She doesn't even have a car, which is why I drove her to the gym today," Steve told me.

Without warning, "the intern" appeared from behind the Stairmaster. Blonde, stacked, and slim in a pair of running shorts that was more like an extended thong.

"Ms. Dickinson, I love your work!" she lied. "I used to see you in magazines when I was a child." Then she adjusted her top and smiled sweetly at Steve.

"Aren't you *still* a child?" I asked and everyone began to laugh. Except for me.

"Someday, I'd like a career in front of the camera like you," Maya cooed. "I'm just such a huge fan, Ms. Dickinson. Maybe someday I could ask you a few questions."

Gorgeous. Sweet. Nice.

A total cunt.

"Come over to the house later. We'll provide the movies," Steve repeated. "What is this 'we' crap?" I thought. "Suddenly they're a 'unit'?" Of course, I can't say what I want to, which is: "When's the bitch moving out?" But I did decide in my mind that it was time for Maya to move over and let the Big Dog lick the bowl clean.

Live-in CBs aren't easy to fuck with. They're bottom-feeders, the lowest of the low. They're like subservient Nubian slaves to these men. Naturally, the men love them.

This wasn't going to be easy. But I love a challenge.

On the way home from the gym, I mulled over going to "their house" for our three-way movie date. What if Steve had already cast me as the brunette in a threesome he was directing later? I decided it was up to me to take the upper hand in this mess.

"Steve, it's Janice," I said, calling his cell. "I've thought about tonight, and I don't think it's a good idea. Unless you've put someone up for adoption."

Click.

I knew my indifference would drive him nuts.

Later that afternoon, I re-re-considered my plan after Steve called again and begged me to come over. I decided I would show my face over there and find ways to get rid of the heinous Maya. Men are born to hunt, after all—but that's no reason we women can't take a few shots too.

It was CB season. Lock and load.

Wardrobe was my first weapon. I knocked on the door of Steve's mansion feeling lean and mean in my black Prada miniskirt and Manolos, with a great BCBG low-cut white tank top completing the picture. Three seconds after Steve hugged me, it was on.

Like a dog hearing a Twinkie wrapper somewhere, Maya bounded down the stairs two at a time, and her plan became obvious. She wasn't going to leave us alone for a minute. She was sporting Daisy Dukes so short they should've been called Dukes, a barely-there tank top, and no shoes—as in, "I live here, bitch, and you're just another intruder for me to shove out the door."

Steve kissed me on the cheek and I didn't allow Maya's Target fashion sense to throw me.

Instead, I gave her a dose of her own medicine. If she wanted to be the housegirl, then it was time for her to earn her keep. My plan will work with any CB. You simply treat them as if they were your own personal assistant.

"Maya, honey, would you mind running down to Starbucks for me?" I asked, sugar dripping from my lips. "Would you get me that slow-brew coffee? Make sure they brew it from the grounds up."

Digging into my cute Chanel bag, I tossed her a twenty-dollar bill. "Take your time."

"Oh, okay, Ms. Dickinson, but the traffic is really bad right now," Maya said, biting her full lower lip and looking at her meal ticket for confirmation of her marching orders.

"Well, then, you better leave right now," I said, smiling warmly as I practically shoved her out the door. It's not easy driving barefoot, but they learn that young in the Midwest.

Moments later she returned, without coffee but with a *problem*. CBs always have a laundry list of little, teeny-tiny problems for their man to solve. What you need to do, if you want to win, is anticipate their bullshit. I was already holding out Maya's flip-flops for her when she ran back in. "Now run along, sweetie," I said, slamming the door. "Drive safely!"

Steve seemed amused, but I needed to wipe the smile from his face and fast. I told him about my own (imaginary) houseboy, Ramon, who did so much for me when I was hard up for an extra pair of hands around the house.

"Ramon gardens, takes out the trash, makes my bed," I rambled on.

"How old is Ramon?" Steve asked, sounding a little perturbed.

"Oh, he's twenty. He was on a soap in Mexico, but then there was that huge scandal with the nude pictures of him. He doesn't have a car. I just love to help out—just like you do, Steve."

Steve was speechless. It was shaping up to be better than any movie we could end up watching.

An hour later, we were cuddled up close on the couch, watching *Kill Bill*, when the front door slammed. An extremely agitated Maya huffed through the doors of the screening room holding a cup of freezing cold coffee for me, muttering, "I was in traffic for more than forty-five minutes."

Her skin was shiny, her Daisy Dukes were in a bind, and there was a faint coffee stain on her tank top.

"You are such a lifesaver," I told her, smiling up at her like we were long-lost sisters.

"Any time, Janice," she sneered.

"Really?" I asked innocently.

"Whatever you need," Steve said, tracing his fingers in circles around my knee.

"Well, I hate to be awful, but, Maya, could you run down to the Rite-Aid and buy me some Tampax?" I said. "Slender."

Steve's eyes popped at that last, carefully chosen word. You don't want your guy thinking you're the size of the Grand Canyon.

Sneaking a glance at Maya, I noticed that her eyes were wide with horror.

"But I'm sure I have some tampons," she offered, looking like another road trip would send her over the edge.

"My vagina is very particular," I replied, as if I were cursed with the tightest little jewel box in Beverly Hills.

Yes, girls, you can send the CBs on errands that take a long time. Do it in the middle of rush hour. Ask for the impossible. Whatever you do, just get rid of them. Rehearse these words: "Listen, can I trouble you . . . again?" After Maya got back, I sent her out again to get me some regular Tampax, insisting that I'd never asked for slender—she must have misheard me.

CBs will do your bidding, because they lack the household authority to get all up in your face. It's easy to kill them with kindness. "So sorry to ask, but could you please drop by my place and bring me whatever mail's in the box? If it's not there yet, could you wait a while until it arrives?"

CBs have a way of reappearing.

Two days later at the gym (no, I didn't sleep with Steve—I was taking it slow, digging my heels until I knew I'd outlast Maya or Steve would never get any), I saw him and waved. A split-second later, Maya made her presence known, bouncing over in her new leotard.

"Steve, I'm ready to go whenever you're ready," she said in a breathless tone designed to suggest the precursor to an orgasm.

"I'm busy here," Steve said, rebuffing her to talk to me. Glancing at Maya, I saw her eyes narrow. If she'd had her fingers around a five-pound hand weight at that moment, I realized, she'd have murdered me with it.

"What's up with you and Maya?" I finally asked Steve after she stomped off.

"Well, she just stays in my guest room," he said. "It's no big deal. I'm just guiding her career. She wants to be an actress."

"Oh, you're guiding her?" I said. *Right over to your penis*, I thought. I was pretty sure Maya could find her own way.

"Remember, she doesn't have a car or an apartment. She's from Germany," he said, as though she were a humble foreign-exchange student on a world peace tour. I never heard an accent.

"Oh, she doesn't have anything?" I said. *Except a pussy*, I thought.

Steve suggested that I might like to come over for another movie night; this time, he thought, maybe I could even cook dinner for them. I was pissed. Why should I cook for him *and* the CB? How many more errands was I supposed to dream up for her?

When that night rolled around, though, I skipped it. I didn't even answer Steve's calls. I didn't need to say anything; he was getting the message. He voice mailed me the next morning after not seeing me at the gym. "Janice, why aren't you calling me back? Are you okay?"

I waited a few hours and returned the call. Between my book, VH1, and my upcoming trip to South Africa, I complained, I was *oh* so busy. "I'm horny, too, but I guess that'll have to wait," I said. Men go crazy when you talk about sex bluntly, like it's just another thing on the to-do list. Because for them, it is.

Putting my hand lightly over the receiver, I said loudly, "Ramon, Ramon! Yes, bring those fresh-cut flowers in here." Then I clicked off on Steve.

Two days later, the phone rang. It was Steve again. "Janice, what if we went out for breakfast? Just the two of us."

Yes, he'd gotten the message. He may have been a director, but I was the producer.

There was no room in this relationship for a CB. He was beginning to resent Maya, I could tell: She was the only thing standing between him and what he wanted from me.

"I'd have you over, but it's tough with Maya leaving her shit all over the place," he griped.

"Children can be messy," I mused. I thought of suggesting that he should get someone from SAG to baby-sit her, but I refrained. This was no time to bring her up again. All I needed to do was sit back and enjoy the eventual ousting of the CB.

Obsession. Compulsion. I was trying not to get into those traps with Steve, but I really did like the guy. We went to breakfast at a nice French bistro on Sunset. As I sat staring across the table at Steve's dreamy self—like a Greek god with the hair of a surfer dude—I wondered: *Why am I always so attracted to a guy on a mission?* It was just a few weeks before the presidential election, and Steve wanted to rent vans and take black voters to the polls in Florida to vote for John Kerry.

"Why don't we fly to Florida and organize a bus to help people vote?" Steve suggested.

All I heard was the "we."

"What about some tastefully decorated Greyhound buses?" I suggested. "If we're going to get out the vote, everyone should be comfortable."

"Janice, are you really going to South Africa this weekend?" he asked. "Maybe I could visit? I don't really have plans."

Here was a man with a mission—and no plans for the weekend. I was in love.

"I could buy you a ticket to South Africa," I suggested. Eventually, you have to let the man know where you stand.

We wandered back to the gym for our post-breakfast workouts. Then, from out of nowhere, Maya appeared. For a moment my anger flared; *Do I have to start carrying a bug zapper?* I wondered.

Once more, I chose the best course of action—ignoring her. I turned to the man who was making my heart beat and said, "I'm gonna skip the workout. Why don't you walk me out?"

He walked me down the street and to my car. On the way, he mentioned that Maya was going back to Germany that week. He was all done guiding her and was setting her free to tackle the big, bad world.

I knew she'd be a big hit wherever her vagina took her.

"Want to do this again tomorrow?" Steve asked me.

"Lunch, dinner, or both?" (It's always best to have a plan that's detailed but flexible.)

When we got to my car, I stood there with the wind in my hair. I was wearing an army-green jacket, skin-tight pants, and my Nikes. Steve put his arms around me and I pushed my nose into his neck.

Inhale. Exhale. I did it deeply, and it unnerved him.

He smelled delicious.

Steve kissed me twice. One cheek and then the other. Then he went for the lips. I love a guy with ambition.

Before I left, I gave him another deep sniff. And as we walked away, he waved and I blew a kiss. It was all very Hollywood-romantic—now that it was officially just the two of us.

And what happened to the CB? She's probably searching for her next home. The moral of this story is that you have to be more intelligent and quicker than any CB, whether she comes in the form of a hot housegirl, a nosy mother, a protective ex, or anyone else who would try to deprive you of your goal.

Lesson 35

Telephones Make Excellent G-Spots

THE ANCHORMAN ALWAYS RINGS TWICE

Imagine being on a desert island with a handsome and successful anchorman. I can't name this person, but by the time this book comes out you might know from the photos in the tabloids. Let's just say that this man is very handsome and recently divorced. He's a hot commodity who just came on the market, and I've had my eye on him ever since we met at a school function.

I could barely look at him without thinking, "Kiss, kiss, kiss."

His look said, "More, more, more."

The pluses: This guy is my age and perfect for my demographic. He's got a great job and a hot ass. He's got a huge ego, which can be attractive.

"I control the press," he told me in the school parking lot. How's *that* for an ego? I appreciate confidence.

After he left that night, one of the other moms approached me and said, "I hear that he sleeps around."

I frowned at this feeble and pointless cock-blocking effort, but deep down I was thinking, "You should sleep around a little bit, too, Sweetie."

"He's a groper," another mom told me.

"I hope so," I thought.

What did I do next? What have I been telling you, for years now? *NOTHING!*

You see them. You talk to them. You do nothing.

They must come to you.

Trust that it will happen. If you do, they will—every time.

One night, Anchorman called me out of the blue. My caller ID told me the call was coming from Florida, but that gave me no idea who it could be. Maybe some cute guy who wanted to invite me to his beach house for a weekend of fun in the sun? That sounded good—except for the cold I was fighting, which was threatening to upgrade to pneumonia. Net result: When I picked up the phone, I sounded like a drag queen emceeing a Demi Moore lookalike contest.

"Did you miss me?" Anchorman asked with that smooth airwaves-ready voice.

He was at the Super Bowl, and while he was sitting alone in his hotel room, all thoughts had led to Janice. That was cute, but I couldn't figure out how he had gotten my digits. He insisted he'd searched the school directory until he found my phone number. Never have I been so glad that I joined the damned PTA.

I felt like I was dying, but I wasn't yet dead.

"Oh, you want to swim with this great white shark?" I ask, chomping my teeth flirtatiously into the receiver.

"That's a great line," he responded. "I know how to swim, too."

It was 10:00 P.M. and he had had a few drinks with the rest of the guy reporters, but he wasn't too drunk to turn on some charm.

"You sound like you have a terrible cold," he observed, sounding terribly concerned.

"Yeah, I'm sick," I confirmed, but I didn't dwell on it. (If you want sympathy, call your girlfriends. Men don't want to hear about your aches and pains, even if they're the biggest whiners around themselves.)

Anchorman didn't want to discuss anything but his own symptom—a big ache down below. "What are you wearing?" he asked. So much for all the concern in his voice—unless he was just worried that I wasn't wearing enough warm clothing to get through my bronchitis.

"Leopard panties and a black bra," I said. "And Chanel No. 5," Exactly what he wanted to hear. "What are *you* wearing?"

"Nothing," he reported.

"I'm taking off the panties," I responded. "It's either the fever or your voice. I'm not so sure yet, but we'll see in a few minutes. Oops, they're soaking wet."

On the other end of the phone line, I could hear a deep intake of breath. I'd been here before with other men, but like a favorite restaurant, it was always worth another visit. I knew by the ragged sound of his breathing that it was okay for me to take the lead.

"You know you want me," I said while he continued to pant. "If I were you, I'd be happy to be on the phone with me, too, because I'm so horny I could do anything."

If you're going to try your hand at phone sex, you have to *sell* it. You can't hesitate. Just open your mouth and let all the nasty stuff come out. Say it with total conviction. When you're good at it, you could read a grocery list and the guy would still bug out.

"What do you really want?" he finally asked in a breathless, disturbed, very deep voice.

"From you, all I want is sex," I moaned. "I don't want anything from you but cock in my box." So sue me. It's the first thing that came to mind. It's okay to say things you don't really mean during phone sex. It's all for a response. You don't actually have to follow through with your phone-sex promises. Men are the same way: When they jerk off, they think about crazy stuff they would never really do. You're giving voice to that. Try it, and I bet you'll get carried along on the wave, too.

The outlandish things you say will either bring out the devil in your listener or he'll laugh you off. It's safe, harmless, and fun, too. For the man who believes that the woman can't hold up her end and might be embarrassed with sexy talk, it's also an eye opener. He's figuring if you're uninhibited on the phone then you must be a hot lay, too. And let's face it—you are.

"You want me for sex. *Everyone* wants me for sex," he was saying, indulging in the rule I just mentioned.

Phone-Sex 101

- HAVE HIM AT "HELLO." IF YOU WANT TO HAVE PHONE SEX, START WITH A VERY BREATHY HELLO. DON'T OVERDO IT. TO CAPTURE THAT HOT-AND-BOTHERED *JE NE SAIS QUOI*, PRETEND YOU'VE JUST WOKEN UP.
- LAY HIM ON THE LINE. AS YOU BEGIN DIRTY TALK, NARROW IN ON ONE ACT HE SEEMS TO ENJOY HEARING ABOUT. PICK A POSITION AND SEE IT TO COMPLETION. IF YOU TALK TOO RANDOMLY, HE'LL TALK FOREVER AND EVER.
- DON'T HOLD BACK. YOU'RE NOT TALKING WITH YOUR MOM. MEN ARE UNSHOCKABLE. IT MIGHT SEEM STUPID IN YOUR HEAD, BUT IF IT'S SEXUAL, JUST BLURT IT OUT. HE'LL LOVE IT.

Top Five Best Answers to "What Are You Wearing?"

(5) "JUST SOME PANTIES." All men are breast men. Plus, "panties" trumps "underwear" when it comes to aural sex.

(4) "A SILKY NIGHTIE." Men love lingerie because it's intimate and was invented to make any woman look like a centerfold.

(3) "I JUST GOT IN—A BEAUTIFUL GOWN AND HIGH HEELS." Heels drive even nonfetishists nuts. Open-toed heels are what Shelley Winters called "fuck-me" shoes.

(2) "MY BIG FLUFFY WHITE ROBE." Some men dig women all

clean and flowery, and a robe creates that image of being freshly showered. Plus, easy access.

---

(1) "NOTHING AT ALL." Guaranteed to make a big splash.

"Come on over then and do me," I offered, knowing he was in Florida, a six-hour flight away from Los Angeles, so he wasn't likely to come pork me on my deathbed or anything.

"What are you wearing?"

"Nothing now," I said and this very famous man started to moan, "Oh, oh, oh . . ."

"Let it fly, baby," I whispered while grabbing something from my nightstand. Not a vibrator—my nail file. I might as well tend to a manicure while talking on the phone. I've always been very good at multitasking. Women take as much pride in their nails as men do in the size of their load.

After he came, he was suddenly very concerned for me again. "We gotta get you better, because I want to see you when I come home. Do you want to go to my doctor?"

It's so sweet when your man has phone sex with you and then passes on valuable contacts.

One note about phone sex: He can't come over afterward, even if he's only a few blocks away. Phone sex is an event within itself. Think about it for a minute: If your guy is past thirty, he's already had an orgasm or two on the phone. If he comes over, he'll probably conk out early; he's already had enough excitement for one night.

And if you get bored with the phone sex, if he's taking forever, remember that there is one sure-fire way to end it immediately *without* saying something rude.

Just say, "Don't you wanna just explode all over my face?"

He'll lose it every single time.

Lesson 36

Homosexuality Goes Both Ways

YOUR BOYFRIEND'S GAY AND IT SUCKS

So many women find themselves dating a guy who—you can't quite put your finger on it. And you've tried! But he won't let you. A little tongue kissing, but no sex? That's a good clue that he might be gay.

Why do gay men pretend they're straight, dating and even marrying women? They're just sad people, these hetero wannabes. I feel sorry for them, because they're pretending to be something they're not.

But you can't worry about his hangups. If you suspect your guy is gay, you have to hang up the phone and don't call back. After all, what are you ever going to get out of it?

I'm still trying to learn this lesson myself, actually. I can't say who it was, but yes, I've dated and mated with a gay man. My gaydar was *so off*. I'd seen gorgeous pictures of this guy, and a friend of mine said, "Oh, I know him. He's gay." It was like the moment in a movie when the police come to the door and say, "Sorry, ma'am—he's dead."

I was like, "Oh, my God—that explains the five times we went to bed and nothing happened . . ."

I was upset—at myself! I really liked him. He was a good dancer, had great taste in clothes, took care of his family—as I think about it now, I realize my gaydar must have been on vacation in Aruba.

Even though it was doomed, though, I really wanted in on that action. I'd date him again. He's one of the only exes I'd date again. I don't recommend dating gay men—the sex is more like humping the couch—but we had fun. If he'd already inherited all his family's money, I guess his flaws wouldn't matter so much.

I guess the real answer is: Don't date a gay man unless you want to have a lot of fun and no sex.

CHIC LESBIAN

I was standing at a bar not drinking—which I always think is a bold statement—when the sexiest man I'd ever seen sidled up to me. He had dark hair and a bright smile that made me think he might be funny as hell if I talked to him.

Bam! Smack! I was in love. I mean heat.

Just when I was thinking about ways to get this guy to make a serious play for me, I felt another pair of eyes staring at me.

It was obvious *I* was someone *else's* Bam! Smack! that night.

I turned to take a discreet look at who was ogling me—and came eyeball to eyeball with a woman. Come to think of it, I had noticed her already, when she'd strategically sat herself ten feet away from me and started teasing me with her eyes. As I looked at her, she pulled these totally useless but very chic sunglasses (indoors!) down and began to give me sizzling fuck-me looks every few seconds as she talked with some guy who was doing the same thing to the man standing next to me.

What was I supposed to do?

In true go-with-the-flow spirit, I gave her a little equal-opportunity flirt back. It was harmless. I love lesbians. They're always all over me like a palmful of body lotion. Let me just say if Kim Basinger came up to me in a club and asked for a kiss, my answer would be, "Okay. Where?" She's *just that hot*. (You say she's straight? I don't care.)

This chic lesbian wasn't up to Kim's standard, but she was worth some eye fencing. If you're curious about sex with a woman, I say go for it. Just treat them better than a man would, or your karma will kill you.

While we're on the topic of lesbians, the other night I allowed my assistant and his gay stylist friends to dress me in drag and take me out to the gay bars. I looked like a man impersonating Uma Thurman in *Pulp Fiction*, with bangs, a fedora, and fierce cat eyes. Honestly, you couldn't tell if I was a woman, a man, or a little of both. I kind of forgot *myself* for a while. They say all the biggest superstars have no gender, but the biggest supermodels need to have both genders at once. I've had both genders . . . have you?

I'm basically a gay man trapped in a woman's body—no offense to TomKat.

We all went to a place in Hollywood across from the Pleasure Chest called the Parlor Club, where I ran into the producer of the hottest fucking show on TV. She wanted to make out with me (producers are used to making insane demands without even saying hello first) and I did kiss her a few times after she swore, "I'm going to put you on my show." (Ah, Hollywood, it never changes. Except now the casting couch is sometimes right out in plain view inside a gay club.)

"I'll shove you into a catfight scene with the series lead," the producer swore, shoving her tongue down my throat. I wasn't that into her tongue, but my mind raced for ideas when it came to the catfight. Maybe I could pull a Janet Jackson and let one boob slip out during the action. Accidentally, of course. I'd have me naked by the end of that scene. This is something I've done on the red carpet, except people were titillated when I did it—as opposed to gagging, as they did when Tara Reid let some nip slip. My breasts are just better: They're fake, and they're spectacular.

A few minutes later, I was out of that club and on my way to a boys-only establishment where this gay director I know was all over me in about three seconds.

"Janice, I'd recognize you anywhere. I'd even go straight for you," he said. I laughed . . . but he didn't.

"We love you, Janice. You're our favorite bitch!" yelled a guy at the bar, giving new meaning to the phrase "screaming queen."

For a minute, I mulled over the idea of turning a gay man straight, but it just seemed too complicated. Lesbians really are easier. So I rounded up my posse and we went to an all-girl bar—after all, I'm nothing if not all girl. A few seconds later, I found myself making out with two lesbians in a corner. There were exposed tits and Cosmos spilling into laps and frustrated cell-phone video directors attempting to pull a Paris Hilton on me. A gaggle of go-go dancers started floating around us, and I realized it was all getting a little out of hand. Whose hand *was* that? Someone stuffed a hundred bucks down my cleavage.

"Cab money," I told myself.

"I'm afraid to take you home," one of the lesbians lamented to me loudly. "You'll steal my girlfriend." As if I were a done deal. I tore away, found my posse, and split before I ended up end-up.

Later that night, I was in a luxury suite at the St. Regis Hotel in Century City. Two stylish designers I ran into earlier had invited me and my assistant to stop by and take a look at the new summer line. These guys dressed Nicole Kidman, so I was interested. In their suite, I saw some racks of Chanel. Sweet suite.

"Janice, you don't remember, but I dressed you for six different shows," one of the stylists told me, "and you're always amazing."

"I'm sure you're right about everything you just said," I replied. "Now let's go Coco loco."

They were amused when I tore my clothes off in a second and dove into the most expensive suit on the rack. If these guys had just blinked, I could've rolled the entire rack into the elevator and then right into my limo, Grinch-style.

At 4:00 A.M., after a night of lesbians, gay men, and *haute couture*, I was ready to go home.

At one point, I had a dream where a handsome man asked if I'd rather sleep with him or own one single new Chanel suit.

Sexy vs. Not Sexy

It's SEXY when a man wants to masturbate in front of you. If he asks, just say, "Go ahead. I'll watch." You can ask him to do the same for you, which will lead to a very hot night, I promise.

It's NOT SEXY when a man masturbates *instead* of doing anything else with you. This is a guy who's too used to his own hand and he needs to wean himself off it. You're not a peep show.

"Which lasts longer?" I asked him in my dream, making more sense asleep than I sometimes do awake.

The truth? I've done the girl-on-girl thing, but I'm not much of a lesbian.

I may not be a dyke, but I'm Coco Chanel's bitch.

Sex Can Be Unavoidable

KARMIC DEBTS

Mick Jagger is the devil—a sex-addict devil. How do I know this? He told me so himself—before we got naked, while we were naked, and after we were naked.

Me: "Mick, where did you get the inspiration for 'Sympathy for the Devil'?"

Mick: "Who do you think you're naked with here, Janice?"

It's always interesting when a man knows himself so well. As for my reaction to sleeping with the devil, I just have to say that I sinned. He was Mick Jagger, for God's sake, and the guy just reeks sexiness. I defy any woman to get this chance with her favorite rock star and demurely say, "You know what? I know you're one of the sexiest rock creatures on the planet, but I have to go home and make a meatloaf tonight for charity."

Get real, ladies. That ain't happening.

Until now, I've been rather demure about exactly what Mick was like in bed. But I owe it to my students of love to let them live vicariously through the Oracle.

First of all, just thinking about Mick in bed while I drive around in my car and dictate this chapter of the book . . . maybe I should pull to the curb before getting into more of the details.

Wandering into my boudoir with Mick, my brain was screaming, "Start me up!" Somehow, I just knew Mick could start me up quickly when he disrobed in about three seconds flat. If there were an Olympic sport for shedding your clothes, Jagger would have scored gold.

I was more fashion challenged: My bright yellow Converse basketball shoes were double-knotted and refused to come off. Not wanting to look like a stooped-over old lady trying to untie her damn shoes, my mind raced for far sexier ways to free my feet. Finally I kicked off one shoe, but I gasped when it landed on top of the crystal chandelier in my bedroom with those fucking laces draping down to mock me. Wanting to kick the other shoe through the window, I wiggled my leg furiously to no avail. The shoe refused to budge, so there was only one solution.

Leaving the damn shoe on, I looked at Mick and jumped into bed.

What the hell? He isn't perfect either, with his one green eye and one brown one. Plus, he was the devil, which is why I now believe his clothes actually unbuttoned themselves.

"I want you to 'ave my bay-bee," he whispered in the dark.

Demonspawn.

I ignored my worries about forked-tongue offspring when Mick got down to business.

Imagine two Big Dogs tangled together in a lusty dance, with each wanting total domination. Mating with Mick for me was like a boxing match; the ring was my queen-sized mattress. He'd flip me over and then I'd flip him over—which wasn't hard, because he only came up to my shoulders if we were standing.

In the throes of passion, I thought about my ideal man—who was *not* Mick Jagger. My dream was a Jewish Jim Morrison; Mick was more like the Dutch Boy you see on paint cans, with his perfect little haircut. Feeling empowered, I began to realize that I was making a huge exception for Mick; after all, he wasn't at all my type. But then again, it didn't matter—because he was Mick Jagger.

After we made love, he was a talker.

Mick: "Luv, do you wanna see my diamond?" He had a diamond in his tooth.

Me (peering into his mouth with the long tongue): "Mick, all I see is the spinach you had for lunch, which is still stuck in your teeth."

Mick was a skinny guy; he and Iggy Pop both have that famished-chic thing going on. He looked like a prima ballerina in his prime; his thighs were so hard and toned that I started to worry about my own.

Sometimes you just have to fuck a guy, even if he's not your type. Especially if he's Mick Jagger. It's chemical. It's a karmic debt.

Don't Do Kinky Shit . . . Unless You Want To

UNSAFE AT ANY SPEED

I don't have all the answers, but two things I know for sure: If you go out and let someone fuck you without a condom, eventually you're going to get a disease. And if you swim in the sea with your period, you're going to get eaten by sharks.

Use a fucking condom.

Use a condom fucking.

NIP/FUCK

The other day, I made a visit to one of the most important men in my life. He's closer to my heart than any boyfriend, ex-boyfriend, agent, lawyer, or even potential billionaire who might choose to retire me to the Caribbean island he owns.

I'm talking about my plastic surgeon, the extraordinary Dr. Frank Ryan of Beverly Hills. Dr. Frank is the plastic surgeon who keeps his own lips zipped about who he's done, but Vince Neil is on the record that he did his fabulous new face for him. He's also the guy Nicolette

Sheridan went to when the press called her "a little transgendered-esque" and accused her of having work done: Dr. Frank examined her face and pronounced her scar-free.

My face is scar-free, too, but that's because Dr. Frank does great work. I have to admit that I have a tiny crush on him and fantasize about operating on *him* sometime. I also love teasing him about how rich he's gotten by lifting half of Beverly Hills. Once, joking with him, I asked to borrow his credit card. He whipped out his John Deere credit card and said, "Honey, spend as much as you want."

I didn't find it funny.

Still, Dr. Frank is one of my team, which is why I share the major events in my life with him. Sometimes he's the first to know, because he's just that important.

"Dr. Frank, the E! Channel called and they want to do a *True Hollywood Story* on me. Of course, I want you to be in it," I told him. "I also want you to take a good look at my face and find some way to freshen me up. I'm going to be in millions of homes. I don't want them to see lines."

"You're getting a bit crinkly under the eyes again," Dr. Frank said.

"You don't have to be nasty," I replied. But he's the only man who's allowed to agree with me when I say I need work.

By the way, it's not my fault that I have a few lines. I have a busy life: With all my duties raising my kids, feeding my dogs, tending to my boyfriends, remaining the party animal of the universe, keeping up with my tranny and gay friends, staying fashionable, holding court on TV, writing books, developing new ideas, dealing with exes—I've earned my lines. But they're mine, so I can choose what to do with them. I give them the big thumbs-down, *Gladiator*-style.

After a short examination and then some deep thinking, Dr. Frank asked a crucial question: "You don't have any shoots for the next four or five days, do you, Janice?"

I shook my head because the rest of the week was camera-free.

"We can do an acid peel under your eyes," Dr. Frank said in a matter-of-fact voice. I had no idea what he was talking about, so he gave me a few particulars.

"It's going to sting," he warned.

"I've had a broken heart. I've dated a married guy. I delivered two children vaginally. I can handle pain," I informed him.

Dr. Frank walked away to stir up some of his magic brew.

"Bring it on!" I yelled to him.

And without further ado, I was suddenly in a chair and he was dipping a big Q-tip into some liquid concoction that appeared to be smoking. I don't know what its active ingredient was—eye of newt?—but let me tell you, when he dabbed on my acid peel, I jammed my Dolce & Gabbana boots so hard into Dr. Frank's floors that I think I hit bedrock. Pain! I'd never felt such hurt in my life. It stung so much, my vagina actually hurt from clenching. It was as if ten million bees had landed in and around my eyes and started stinging me for pleasure.

I canceled the rest of my day, including a meeting with Benny Medina, who used to manage J-Lo and could have been helpful to J-Dick. When my boyfriend called to ask me out to dinner, for a split second, I thought about just curling up alone in bed that night. But the Big Dog hates to turn down a night out of the kennel, so I accepted.

At home before the date, I tried out every cover-up in the universe—and then went right for the heavy stuff. Gobbing the Dermablend out of the jar, I caked it on. But I knew the far better trick was putting on my sexiest pink La Perla bra and undies. Ladies, if you have a skin problem, a lift situation, or even a nasty zit, the key is to distract the men from your face and onto your breasts. If you play it right, the men will never take their eyes off your boobs. You could be a two-headed Siamese twin, but as long as you have breasts, you're in business.

It was one of those fabulous romantic dinners where everyone is in great spirits. My boyfriend insisted it was my congratulatory dinner for getting a small role in an upcoming movie.

In the middle of this love fest, Cuba Gooding Jr. stopped by to pay his respects to the world's first supermodel. I officially love the black man. He had me at hello.

The presence of a movie star heightened my already high mood, and my date was enjoying shooting the shit with an Oscar winner. As much as I'd love to do a love scene with Cuba, I never stopped paying attention to my gorgeous date. We had true balance.

It was dark when we drove home and even darker in my bedroom when we made love. Suddenly, my eyes stopped hurting. An orgasm is like morphine in that way. Several are even better.

The next morning, I was thinking about the idea of having the kind of hot sex you can only have after the sun rises. Lifting my head off the pillow, I gazed at my sleepy boyfriend—and he suddenly jumped twenty-five feet out of the bed.

"WHAT—!" he screamed. "WHAT HAPPENED TO YOU?!"

For a split second, I was hurt and confused; my come-hither gaze seemed to be having a Medusa effect. Usually, it works wonders. And then, like in a bad movie, I could hear Dr. Frank's warnings.

Vaulting out of bed, I ran into the bathroom to see what had happened to me.

The news wasn't pretty, and frankly, neither was I. My eyes were surrounded by thick black circles; I looked like a raccoon in a nightie. My eyes were two black holes. The acid is like having third degree burns around your eyes. I didn't realize my skin would be quite so well done.

"I gotta go," said my gallant bedmate, looking away as he tried to kiss me on the lips. He missed and sort of barely kissed the side of my head, far from the barbecue.

"Oh, fine, walk away," I cried.

"I have to work," he said, trying to calm down, but he winced when he looked at me. Even my tears weren't bringing him around.

"My life is over," I thought.

An hour later, I was at a café in Beverly Hills with huge Jackie O sunglasses on. I looked like a woman who'd been beaten up and was hiding it. Suddenly, I began to sob. I wasn't necessarily crying for myself, I was sobbing for every single person who has ever felt rejected or abandoned or . . . ugly.

I sob for burn victims. I also sob for everyone who has never been on the cover of *Vogue* or thinks they couldn't be. I sob for women who don't realize that they're beautiful and only look at the flaws in themselves.

There are flaws, and then there was my extra-crispy face.

Despondent, I called Dr. Frank, accusing him like a scorned lover. "What the hell?" I said.

"I asked if you were working for the next few days," he responded. He knows me too well to get frustrated with my moods.

"I said I wasn't *working*. I *am* living through the next few days. I *do* have a horny boyfriend."

"It will only get better," Dr. Frank says. He always tells is like it is, so I tend to believe him when he explains each process to me ten times, and informs me that everything is happening that should happen—that I'm not a freak lab accident.

In my car, I lathered on about fourteen inches of makeup over my eyes so I could show my face in my yoga class without the mat-bitches knowing about my peel. Switching to even better Chanel glasses, I drove around. I knew people were probably thinking I was hung over. The joke was on them: I didn't even have a headache.

"Cancel my meetings," I told my assistant. "I don't wasn't anyone seeing me like this. I don't want to be seen ever again."

There's a moral to this story. What do you do if you have bruises, scabs, zits, crabs, a herpes flare-up, ten unwelcome pounds, a bad haircut from a Nazi hairdresser, a pair of eyes burned up during plastic surgery? How do you live through the healing process?

You start by not wallowing in pity—for long, anyway. You get out of the house, because changing your environment is key. If you can't leave the house, you distract yourself by cleaning your drawers, getting your accounting together, mowing the lawn, planting spring bulbs, or taking the dog for a walk. Give your old clothes to a woman's shelter.

Shift the focus. Flip it on yourself. Just get out of your head—it doesn't matter how.

I just want you to know that the world's first supermodel feels ugly sometimes.

I consoled myself by turning my pity on my boyfriend. In a few days, I'd look even younger than he does. Before long, I realized I'd swim in a vat of acid if it took off the wrinkles.

I was reminded of the late, great Andy Warhol, who was leaving a funeral one day and said, "I feel really bad for the family, but did you see how great the makeup looked?"

THE CORE OF THE BIG APPLE

Once upon a time, I was holding court at a very big-deal party at the hot nightspot Butter in New York City. There I was, a forty-eight-year-old supermodel, in the most exciting city on the planet, in a posh lounge, surrounded by people tripping over themselves telling me how fucking fabulous I looked. What could possibly be wrong with this picture?

Instead of enjoying myself, I turned my baby browns toward my old publicist friend Nora, who immediately ran over in her Manolo Blahniks to participate in the requisite double-cheek air kisses.

The look of concern on Nora's face told me what I was afraid of: that I looked a little sad, lost, perhaps even a tad depressed. Nobody likes a sad supermodel; the very sight makes people wonder, "What could possibly upset her so much that it wipes out everything else in her amazing life?"

It was Nora's job to make sure everyone was fed, watered, and at least pretending to enjoy themselves. "Janice, what can I get you?" she asked, prepared to offer me anything my heart desired. "A Perrier? A no-carb bacon and lettuce wrap?"

"I don't want a drink or a snack," I pouted. "I want a horny six-foot billionaire who makes me laugh. Do you have one handy?" And just like that, I ordered up an ideal man as matter-of-factly as ordering greens in place of my fries at brunch. Except this was more than a side dish—I was craving a three-course meal: hot, sparkling personality, and loaded. In my profession, you don't get to overeat, so sue me if my appetite worked itself out in other arenas.

It's 2006—why *can't* we just cut to the chase already?

Ladies, we all know that working is overrated, struggling to find happiness is a bore, and the dating scene is about as much fun as giving yourself a Brazilian bikini wax with bubblegum and tweezers. Then again, a girl can never lose hope; after all, just when you least expect it, your fairy godmother might actually turn up.

"Hmmm . . . a billionaire. I think I've got one of those in the back," said Nora, a woman who gave new meaning to the word public relations. She seemed to have a man for every occasion. She was like a mate caterer, and she always had plenty of hot dishes on the menu.

Ten minutes later, Nora sauntered by again and gave me the low-down on the catch of the day. He definitely seemed to have all the right ingredients.

"Janice, I only *sort of* know him, but he does have a spread in East Hampton. Pharmaceuticals, honey," Nora said conspiratorially.

Having a former chemical problem myself, my heart instantly started to palpitate. All I could think of was three little words: "Free BOTOX forever." Nora pointed him out and I sized him up like a jail-bird spying his first steak after getting sprung. Careful, Big Dog—it's never good to let them see you pant.

In my simple black Prada cocktail dress (five thousand bucks never looked so good), I sashayed up to Mr. Free Drugs casually—only to find him standing strangely alone in front of a speaker that was pumping loud rap music in his face. Speaking of loud and in-your-face, he seemed to like what he saw when he gave me the quick size-up, his eyes taking me all in. I opened a new document in my brain, and entered the following information: He was wearing the hell out of a dashing black Armani suit; sporting a deep, real suntan; and had a jiggly neck (time for a little nip/tuck) . . . well, nobody's perfect.

We hadn't exchanged a single word, yet this obviously been-there, done-her man in his fifties was flashing me a boyish grin.

We made it through some small talk and quickly exchanged phone numbers. It was like we were afraid that if we didn't we might get separated and never see each other again. After I penned the seventh digit on the back of his business card, I did the most logical thing under the circumstances. I did what you should do the next time you meet a man you have instant chemistry with.

"I'll be right back," I murmured. And then I left him there and *didn't come back.*

Instead I planted myself at the bar in this club, which was crammed like the bottom hull of the *Titanic* when they locked the steerage class travelers inside to drown. Before long, claustrophobia was starting to kick my ass, so I did an Axl Rose and side-stepped as many people as possible to get to the front of Fun Central. There I found my old friend Paul from *Harper's Bazaar.* Finally, a friendly, safe face in a room full of the drunk and needy. Paul and I were twenty minutes into catching up when Mr. Free Botox wandered by. His jaw hit the floor so hard I thought we'd need to call 911, or at the very least get him a good plastic surgeon (who could have also worked on that neck).

"I thought you left," he said, sounding rather hurt.

"I was leaving, but I had to give in to popular demand and stick around." As planned, it sparked his jealousy; he looked hard into my eyes and said, "I'll give you a call. First thing in the morning. You *will* be home, correct?"

"If I can ever get out of here," I said, touching Paul's sleeve lightly. It might sound a bit manipulative, but trust me—he hardly minded being a pawn in my game of high-stakes (and high-finance) love. Mr. Free BOTOX called the next morning at 9:00 sharp. He was obviously so agitated from meeting me the night before that when he'd written his number for me, it had turned out to be a totally unreadable scrawl. Funny, I thought doctors were the ones with bad penmanship, and pharmacists were the ones stuck deciphering it. He's lucky he called me, because if I'd gotten the urge to call him, I might have gotten a pizza place instead. (Supermodels don't do pizza—only pizza delivery boys.)

I had to admit, I liked the guy's follow-through. *This guy has some potential.*

"Meet me at Elaine's for my book signing," I suggested. I was making an appearance to sign copies of my bestselling book *Everything About Me Is Fake . . . And I'm Perfect.*

Now it was Mr. FB's turn to play hard to get. He balked at joining me as I signed books for a few hundred of my closest fans; instead, he suggested drinks at his place.

That night, after the signing, I threw caution to the remnants of whatever hurricane du jour was roaring through the streets of New York and went up to the penthouse of his very chic building on the Upper West Side.

Then I proceeded to watch him chop coke for the next hour.

What was a recovering addict to do but will herself to resist while staring into the increasingly glassy eyes of the billionaire who was supposed to keep her frownless and in Prada for the rest of her life?

"You have to sew up this deal in the next two months, Janice," I told myself. "You can try to get him to ditch the coke. He's worth it. He's a fucking billionaire. What's one little bad habit? Some men leave socks in the sink. That would be just as hard to take."

But Mr. Free BOTOX turned out to have other shortcomings—to put it mildly. As he got progressively higher and higher, his "don't tell too much" switch got turned off—and he became downright sloppy in his verbal discourse.

"And I really like to stick Swarovski crystal belts up my ass. It gets me off," he mumbled as if he were talking about the weather.

Hello! Or maybe that should have been: Goodbye!

"I also like cock," he slurred. The only thing less appealing than

finding out your date enjoys Swarovski crystal belts up his ass is finding
out that dick is his runner-up choice.

"Me too," I said quickly. See? We had something in common. I
leaned forward in my Marc Jacobs couture dress, letting my breasts fall
out nicely for a quick public viewing. Mr. Free BOTOX stared hard at
the display, but they didn't keep him from continuing his Christmas
wish list.

"I also love threesomes and orgies," he continued. "What about
you, Baby Doll?"

Popping my boobs back into place—you don't need to sweat ele-
gance when the guy is slumped over a stack of cocaine—I said, "Orgies?
Not if I can help it. I'm a supermodel. Come on—we like center stage."

He nodded as if this made perfect sense, did another line of blow
and asked, "Do you like chains?"

"Sure, if you're talking about gold ones from Harry Winston," I
replied, scolding myself for being so unwilling to attend a quick threesome if it could lead to a solid-gold pension.

He proceeded to tell me that he also liked to put chains inside himself and his partners. He also liked them with the same high-end crystals attached. For a split second, I had to give him props for those
crystals—that detail, however insane, appealed to my fashionista instincts. I took a cold sip of Evian to launch my mind back to reality.

After my initial attraction to him and his cash, I was burning mad
at the injustice of it all. No matter how rich he was, I knew there wasn't
enough jewelry cleaner in the world to shine up those crystals after
they'd taken a trip of the type he was describing.

We kissed a few times, but never made it to the gold-metal events he
had in mind. Later that night, we made our way to the release party for
one of Mariah Carey's pre-comeback albums at Lotus. But the thrill
was gone: I didn't need a fairy godmother to tell me to stay away from
coke-snorting freaks who dream of chains and poles.

In such situations, there's only one response. It's an age-old expression that's better than a verbal diatribe or tears or a long discussion of

what went wrong or what could have been—especially when you're dealing with the buffet of men out there:

Who has the time?

"Baby, I want to see you again," whispered Mr. Free BOTOX as Mariah's voice threatened to shatter glass in the background. Quick thought: *I hope he doesn't have any crystal up his ass when she hits that high note.*

I just shook my head and watched all those dollars fly right out of my life. But I had no choice.

"Check, please," I said.

THE CHOKE'S ON YOU

Rocker Michael Hutchence of INXS was a handsome party animal who died in 1997 after hanging himself. Word has it that he was into ropes because the guy liked strangulation sex with famous models—but not this model. I'm not into that kind of stuff. It doesn't even sound hot to me; after all, you can't be sexy if you're dead. (Oh, by the way, all the moisturizer in the world doesn't remove rope burns either. See what I mean? It's a lose-lose situation.)

My two cents? Stay away from autoerotic asphyxiation like the plague. I'm not even sure why anyone ever thought this would be sexy, though I guess it does bring a certain danger to the bedroom. But isn't that room dangerous enough without having to worry that some man might cut off your windpipe for good while he's out of his mind and about to explode? Think about how often a blow job has gone into overtime and you're practically checking your watch; now imagine yourself holding your breath completely during that same time frame.

When it comes to sex, I like it no strings attached.

There was one handsome actor who tried to pull a rope trick on me once. We were macking like crazy, and suddenly he was holding the kind of rope that made me think we were going to lasso a cow out in the range after making it.

Basically, I told him I'd break his wrist if he didn't put his stupid rope back in the drawer. We broke up about five minutes later; then he started dating another supermodel who made many headlines for her relationship with him. I always checked her photos for neck burns—and I saw quite a few, until she broke up with him a while later.

The whole subject makes me gag.

TYING ONE ON

I know plenty of people out there are into bondage, but it just doesn't work for me. See, I'm not as outrageous as people think. Well . . .

First of all, scarves are expensive—the gorgeous Hermès kind I like, anyway—and I don't want bodily fluids on them. It's tough to explain those stains to your dry cleaner.

Second, I think the whole idea of being tied up or blindfolded is a little scary. You're helpless, and I never like to feel that way no matter if it turns a man on or not. Many men will try this, but unless it sounds like the hottest thing in the world to you, tell them to forget it. They'll suggest it, you'll say no. Move on.

It's like hearing that it's fine to wear Uggs with skirts. I'm sure it's fine, but I'm still not doing it.

If you're as wary of ropes and chains as I am, just learn how to bump and grind without the ropes. I know you're thinking, "I bet you've tried this in the past. And with some famous guy." Well, you got me there.

I remember when Frank Zappa whipped out a cord on our date. At first I admired him. "Nice red velvet cord, Frank," I said, thinking it was a cool accessory or something. It was the seventies, after all.

"We can do really great things with this, Janice," he said, twirling the red velvet through the air and trying to nuzzle my neck at the same time.

It dawned on me what the creative genius had in mind and I firmly said, "No way."

Yes, his left eyebrow shot up as if he were disappointed. At that moment I wanted to wrap that red velvet rope around that enormous nose of his, but I guess that wouldn't have been too romantic.

By the way, Frank got over his depression over my nixing the rope. It was a nice try, but he was man enough to accept it when he was denied and life went on.

Bondage always scares me. I don't want to be trussed up, unless it's in some Mugler or Gaultier contraption. And even *then*. . . .

Supermodels are like unicorns—they don't like being harnessed or controlled.

HOW TO PISS ME OFF

We're all adults here. Let's tell it like it is—that's what I'm famous for. (That and my legs.)

There are men out there who find peeing or pooping on their dates to be the ultimate turn-on. I'm rolling my eyes right now just thinking about it. As a germophobe, I'm completely grossed out by these requests.

A producer once asked me, "Janice, are you into fecal matter?" I looked at him with a blank stare and then tossed my drink on him.

Ever persistent, he tried to explain the joys of scat, so I thought he might like something to go with my drink all over his lap. Dumping three meatballs from a buffet onto his crotch, I said, "Eat shit and die." Then I walked away, knowing that those meatball stains would never come out of his fawn Armani pants.

By the way, I told as many people as possible about his freaky requests. It's up to those in the know to out these people, so that unsuspecting women won't fall in love with them and find themselves being asked to make like a toilet when they least expect it.

As for the maniacs who believe golden showers are the way to go, I think they should be spanked. They invoke my anger issues. One night, I right-hooked a guy who suggested that his greatest turn-on would be if he painted me and my bedroom yellow. He thought I had a problem when I told him to piss off.

Unfortunately, I think he got off on that last comment.

Listen to me carefully—the only gold I want to be showered with is twenty-four carat.

VELVET FOG

There is an extremely rich financier in New York City whom I'll call Rich—it's easy to remember. The man likes to throw parties at his house because the place is like a fucking amusement park. First of all, there are endless floors to his Upper East Side home—you could get *lost* just walking from one room to another.

Rich doesn't mind a woman's taking a wrong turn and ending up in the bedroom.

Just in case you're not sure if you want to sleep with him, though, he will cloud your mind a bit. I don't mean that he pushes drugs. The man seduces with his giant fog machine. He actually insists on closing all the windows in the house and smoking the place up, to the point where his guests can't even see each other.

I wasn't ready to have foggy sex with Rich, but I was interested in his unconventional methods of romance. Did women really like the idea of having sex in a room so fogged you couldn't see the walls? Did women reach out into the clouds and grab something they wouldn't when skies were clear? Maybe he thought aesthetics were tired and sex should be all about touch and smell and taste.

Or maybe Rich was just a horndog with a small dick he didn't want anyone to see.

My friend eventually had sex with him, despite my fog advisory. It was okay, she said; a little ouch, and no great orgasm, but okay. She mentioned that Rich had irritating stubble all over his clumsily waxed genitals. Did he think the fog meant he could ignore grooming? If you have to rely solely on your sense of touch, stubble would be more annoying, not less. Maybe he was hiding a big herpes sore, too. Who knows?

Rich left my girlfriend a text message the next day: "I had a good time. I'm going to work. Come over later."

She never replied.

If a man tries to cover up his shortcomings with a smokescreen, call for the check. If what you see is what you get and you see nothing—do the math.

CLOSET CASE

I'm not talking about covert gay men; I'm talking about checking the actual closet before you do it.

One legit film producer bragged to me that a close friend of his—a Hollywood heartthrob turned respected actor who is a household name—was screwing a hot, blond, pretentious model, and he let his friends watch through the closet. How did he know? He knew because he was one of the friends. Girls and boys, check the closet before you do the nasty-nasty.

This same rule applies to suspicious sex encounters that take place near a computer. You guys have heard of webcams, right? Well, you could be the floor show if you don't watch out. Keep an eye out for that little red light: If the guy seems to be performing, or tries to keep you in a certain spot, do a sweep of the room—you don't want to end up being Paris Hilton without the money and career.

SEX TOYS

I remember attending Stephanie Seymour's wedding to the gorgeous polo-playing mogul Peter Brant. Naomi Campbell was there, and she told me that she had brought gag gifts for everyone. Handing me a gigantic dildo, Naomi just stood there smiling—which I thought was awfully strange. Did she want me to use it on her? Right there at the lavish reception? I know Naomi is always hard up for gossip items, but this was going to the extreme.

Luckily, Naomi didn't want a quickie. The dildos were just a rather weird shower gift she forgot to give everyone two days earlier at the bridal shower. Hasn't this woman ever heard of potpourri?

As for sex toys, it's up to you. In general, I recommend body parts that are *attached* to something, instead of inanimate objects.

JEALOUS BITCHES IN HEAT, THREE-WAYS, AND THAT WASCALLY WABBITT

This might come as a shock, but I'm a jealous bitch. Blame it on the fact that I'm a middle child and need all the attention. The point is, I've spent my life learning how to cope with my jealousy, especially when it comes to the opposite sex.

Say you're at a boyfriend's house and his ex calls. This is not the time to grab the phone and call her a skanky bitch who got dumped for a reason. Maybe all of this is true, but you don't need to state the obvious. If you freak out about an encounter like this, you're actually giving the other woman power. Suddenly, your man starts to wonder: If Janice is so worked up, maybe Skanky Sheena was pretty hot . . .

No, no, no!

Back to our scenario. You're at his house and his ex calls.

You: "Hello? Oh, hi, Sheen. How are you? Did you know there's a shoe sale at Neiman's? Hold on. I'll get Antonio. But could you do me a favor?"

Skanky Sheena: "Favor?"

You (urgently): "Could you please *hurry up your conversation,* because we're about to have sex? Okay, thanks. Have a wonderful day."

You pass the phone to your beau—and he hangs up in about three seconds.

Let's say the bitch drops by your boyfriend's house on a Friday night while the two of you are having a romantic dinner at home. She didn't mean to come over (naturally), but she's having a nervous breakdown because their son is having trouble at school. (Exes love to use the kids. I find that rather disgusting.)

You open the door, and before she has time to say anything, you say, "How are you? Do you want to come in and join us for a three-some?"

I did this once, and the woman went running down the driveway.

So what if you come off like a gnarly animal? You've scared the ex, and he's turned on. It's a win-win.

(Of course, the ex could say, "I'd love to do a threesome." Then you simply and quickly retort, "Great—maybe you can hang around when all the others arrive, too." Then you, too, will have the pleasure of watching his ex running down your driveway.)

If you don't, call for the check—because these two have a history Antonio isn't telling you about.

Let's say you're at a club and some bitch is trying to flirt with your boyfriend. This is an easy one: You just get closer to your man and start kissing his neck while staying cool and never acknowledging the babe in heat. Don't give her power. It's tough to keep your emotions in check like this when you want to rip her extensions out, but you gotta keep yourself in control. The one in control wins. Lose control, lose your man.

On the topic of jealousy, I want to warn all of you to enjoy your boyfriends and don't dwell on what *could* happen. Also, don't snoop.

Once someone snooped on me and found my rabbit vibrator. This otherwise-sane individual immediately became jealous of a mechanical sex toy. I replied, "I just bought that so you could find something when you went snooping." Clearly, he was busted.

"But Janice, I tried to turn this rabbit on, and the batteries are dead. You used them until they ran out," my boyfriend retorted.

I don't like accusations. So I dumped the guy and kept the rabbit.

TRANNY LOVE

I'm going to explain a Hollywood Halloween party to you. I was wandering around the yard of the tasteful Hollywood Hills mansion of a designer friend when a handsome Los Angeles businessman did the slow saunter in my direction. It's not that he was hitting on me—we tried that a few times in the nineties, but it didn't take. We're better as just friends.

"Janice, hello. You look beautiful," he said, admiring my costume (Donna Karan wrap skirt and halter top). I was just dropping by this party before a late dinner date. But he didn't care about *my* agenda.

"Why don't you introduce me to your gorgeous friend," he said, staring at the person next to me who was beautiful, black, and in a form-fitting, breast-pouting, silver, Diana Ross gown without pity.

I had to laugh, because my friend happened to have an especially show-stopping accessory inside her outfit—a penis.

"I'd be happy to introduce you to my girlfriend. His name's Stan. Stan's a man. Stan, say hello," I said.

"Hello," Stan purred in his best falsetto voice, a good example of when your best isn't good enough—it came out a bit pitchy. Stan's admirer was very embarrassed, but he looked at Stan and said through tight lips, "You look amazing. Very convincing."

In another corner was another tranny friend in a black velvet robe and a vintage jeweled halter top. He also looked amazing as a she; she might have fooled the same guy if he weren't on guard after that near-miss—especially with the good lighting from the amber candles that were everywhere. His name was Earl and for that night, he'd covered his macho arm tattoos with the drippiest Laura Mercier base makeup. Earl is a brilliant hairstylist to the stars; he now considers himself a recovering tranny.

I have to take a minute to honor the transsexuals of this world. If you're not a tranny and try to pick one up, there's no reason to be embarrassed. Trannies are serious about looking as perfect as, say, a supermodel. I'm the last person to look down on trannies; they have better beauty tips than many stylists I've worked with over the last three decades. Trannies are also very important to the entire social scene, and I love what's happening in West Hollywood every fall. A tranny is born every Halloween. The holiday is an excuse to come out, dress in drag, and embrace a new lifestyle.

On the dating front, trannies have as many problems as the rest of us—more! Trannies have already made a hard life decision to embrace another role each and every day. Their choice can lead to a lifetime of ridicule and misunderstanding.

Of course, the seemingly easy solution is for trannies to date other trannies. But the Oracle can see the pitfalls of two bitches in love. In other words, most trannies aren't lesbians. If "the girls" can work it out, fine. If not, I'd back away during the inevitable explosions such as the day when the last tube of mascara is gone or someone forgot to wax. In most other dating areas, it'd be just too much competition. Whose shoes are those? Who gets the first facial?

Let it be said that despite the obvious cosmetic rivalries, Janice is a defender of trannies. Real trannies are more serious about being women than most women are. I invite trannies to adhere to the love advice I deliver in this book. I'm assuming that many of them want to date straight men, so they're in the same BMW as the rest of us. Like the straight women, I want men to give their trannies a fair shake.

I am born to this cause.

PART IV

Extricating

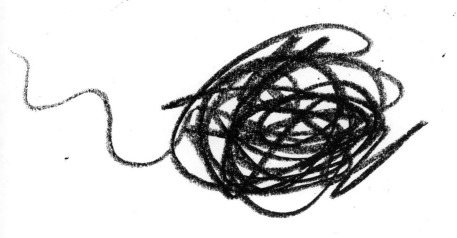

A Crash Course in the Fine Art of Extrication

What's harder than making a date work—or a roll in the hay? Trying to figure out how to make a relationship last. But that's not what I'm here to talk about in this book. People with more authority than I have should try getting that little secret down on paper, and plenty have. I think you just have to keep having new experiences together, travel together, throw yourselves into each other's work. It's important to remain opinionated and to talk about big issues with your partner. Don't tune him out or you'll both pay for it.

You never know what the universe is going to throw you. And that's a good thing. Catch whatever comes together. After all, if you're not willing to try to keep it fresh, then why are you trying to keep it at all?

But this would be a fairy tale if we ended the book with you having had fabulous dates and sex with no sign of an ending. More often than not, what goes up must come down. When it ends, you might feel like ending it all—whether you called things off or he did. But you have to manage a breakup just like you have to manage a relationship. If you know what's coming, you'll be better prepared to manage it.

Retain Mystery Down There or the Check's on You

BETTER DEAD THAN SPREAD

There's a rumor in Hollywood that many A-list actresses adopt children so they won't ruin their perfect size-zero figures. But that's not the story—the whole story, anyway. The truth is, they don't want their men to see them giving birth.

I know childbirth is a beautiful thing, but ladies, you should think twice before you allow your man to see your vagina stretched to the size of the national deficit.

It's normal for pregnancy to blow out your figure, and it's sad to me when I see a man call for the check on a woman during this tender time. That's the lowest of the low (what's up, Billy Crudup?). But I guess the whole madonna/whore thing also sets in. If you're having his child, it's hard for him to see you as his whore in bed. It's a complex subject best left to shrinks—no offense to Scientologists.

A little piece of advice: Think twice about allowing your man in the delivery room, where he'll watch you scream every obscenity known to mankind while you pass what looks like a soccer ball covered in spaghetti out of your private parts. Women are also known to become a little bit possessed while giving birth. Linda Blair in *The Exorcist* was like a student nurse compared to the crazed harpy I became. When I gave birth, I made even the jaded doctors and orderlies around me blush. My OB said, "We never heard a mouth like that. *Ever.*" No wonder my marriage didn't work out.

I don't even blame my then-husband, who watched this hardcore situation go down when my son Nathan was born, for being a bit . . . *conflicted* emotionally about me afterward. He compared it to the scene in *City Slickers* where Billy Crystal pulled that calf Norman out of the mother cow.

What no one tells you is that later, after they see you give birth, men never want to fuck you again. Men in the delivery room? I know it sounds great, ladies, but . . . don't do it. It'll ruin your relationship. Even if you do manage to start having sex again, it'll take a lot of hard work to recapture its former glory.

When it comes to birthing, I believe in privacy. I believe in the old-fashioned approach, where the man drove the woman to the hospital and then went to a local bar to drink cognac and wait for the good news. A few hours later, the man would come back in time to be handed his firstborn son. Afterward, he'd pass out cigars. And soon he was back to having great sex with his wife, fresh from the hospital after spending a month there working on some maximum vaginal healing.

Of course, sometimes you've got to get back on the saddle—especially when your man isn't exactly Johnny-on-the-spot. The day after my daughter, Savvy, was born, I was dancing at the Viper Room. And there were plenty of men there who wanted to dance with me because they never saw me give birth.

It's Okay to Want More, More, More

TRADING UP

I'm sick of reading about my homegirl Jennifer Lopez being dissed for getting married thousands of times. First, let's set the record straight: It's only *hundreds* of times.

No, seriously, she's not exactly Elizabeth Taylor. J-Lo has only been married three times, which is nothing given the level of fame we're talking about here. And there's another, far more important, reason that J-Lo is no Liz: J-Lo only got a Bentley out of Ben. Liz got a museum-quality, cursed diamond out of Richard Burton, among many other baubles—hell, the woman did a book on her trinkets! Let me ask you now: Who is our spiritual marriage leader here? Cars depreciate, but diamonds are forever . . . and they're also for hocking later on to buy nice houses.

By the way, don't forget that J-Lo never even married Ben—which was a good move, because of his aforementioned mineral deficiency. Frankly, I think she would have eventually gotten bored with that pink diamond. Why stop at a teeny pink diamond when you're fucking J-Lo? You should have diamonds in all the colors of the rainbow. J-Lo should have a Bentley full of them so people could be jealous of the rocks that she's got.

The point is, we shouldn't diss women for trading up when it comes to husbands. J-Lo was married to a waiter (!) and then a backup dancer. She's since moved on to a Spanish music star. Can you say upward mobility? I'm not sure why anyone has a problem with this trajectory. It's not like she dumped the backup dancer to get hitched to a dog walker.

Cheating Can Choke Out the Joy Vibe

HOW TO 'FESS UP: "YES, I'M CHEATING"

Love is about the truth. No matter what.

When you lie, you put a bad vibe in the air. Little fibs and white lies are okay. For instance, if your lover is worried about his love handles, you can lie and say you can't see anything. Or, instead, try: "Maybe you'd like to join me at the gym first thing tomorrow morning? Wouldn't it make you feel more confident?" You might break out a Pilates DVD right then and there. Or maybe tell him that the little bit of gray in his hair makes him look like Richard Gere, when he really looks like Wilford Brimley. White lies are expected in any relationship.

What you don't want are the bigger lies—like "I'm *not* having an affair." They will spiral out of control. Once you lie, it's like you're putting a poison cloud in the air. You're spewing out anger into the universe. And I don't care if you're a professional liar, you will act nervous after you lie.

One of the toughest times I've ever had was when I was guilty of having an affair, but wasn't able to tell the man I was dating. Years later, I confessed all to him and even apologized to him, even though we

hadn't been in contact for some time. I did this as part of my alcohol recovery program, and it was a good move. A weight of guilt was lifted
off of me, because this man was treated poorly by me and deserved an
apology.

Was it easy? Hell, no. It was one of the worst moments of my life
when he found me out, and it was damn hard to go back years later and
tell him how I fucked things up.

Sometimes you just have to dive into the hard stuff. You have to
simply say, "I'm sorry. I cheated."

You do this for him. You also do it for your own sanity.

ABORTING THE CHEAT

Let's take a look at Diane Lane in *Unfaithful*. Richard Gere's business
partner saw Diane out with that hottie Olivier Martinez. He ratted Diane out to Richard, who ended up killing her lover. This created worse
problems than infidelity. I'm sure Diane blamed that business guy more
than anyone for her husband's becoming a murderer. It's not rational,
but that's the way it goes in these cases.

By the way, I liked this movie, but did you wonder why anyone
would cheat on Richard Gere? Of course, there's only one plausible answer: She wasn't getting what she needed at home. Obviously, she
wanted to have hot sex in a doorway of a ratty apartment building and
Olivier was more than happy to have give her what she needed, in public places, in the afternoon, before she picked her son up from school.
You can get the country house and the Volvo, but if your man isn't doing you in doorways and dragging you to the backseat for a quick shag,
then he's become complacent and Olivier could strike.

You don't cheat if you're happy with your man or woman. You
don't cheat if you avoid complacency. To that end, hit the Hustler
Store, buy yourself some crotchless undies, put tassels on your nipples
(women and men alike), dip yourself in vanilla-scented oil—try whatever you like, and see if your partner is into it. Take requests.

If you never want to do anything inventive with your partner, then call for the damn check and stop the pain.

The way to abort the cheat (and avoid the home-alone hand job) is to be creative.

WHAT IF HE CHEATS?

It blows our minds when famous men cheat. How could Ethan Hawke cheat on Uma Thurman? We're talking Uma Fucking Thurman! If Uma was my bitch, I'd never cheat on her. Was he nuts or just a man? Maybe both.

What can I say about a man who's cheating? You know when it begins. It starts with those weird phone calls in the middle of the night, unexplained weekends that he can't be around, late nights at work that just don't make sense. You spot a weird charge on the credit card. You see him buying jewelry that you never receive. (This last one is a killer.)

You try to convince yourself that it isn't happening.

It's happening, baby. And you have to deal with it now and not later, when "dealing with it" might mean having the check called on your surprised ass.

Last night I was with a man I love, and his phone rang in the middle of the night. Somebody better be dead if the phone rings past 1:00 A.M. "Who's calling you at three o'clock in the morning?" I demanded, waking from a dead sleep because my instincts told me that I needed answers more than I needed more REM.

"It was an ex who said she needed to hear my voice," said my boyfriend. "How fucked up is that?"

"If that bitch calls again, she better only hear a click," I responded. "Or maybe we should report her to the police for stalking."

He got the message and the phone calls stopped.

It's not that I think he's cheating. He's a good guy. I've also dated men who I've either caught cheating or who have confessed all.

My motto: Once a cheater, always a cheater. If you can't stand the heat, call for the check—immediately.

Years ago, I caught a boyfriend with another woman. "I'm sorry," he explained, "but I cheat. That's just what I do." It's like, "Sorry, judge, but I steal money. That's me." Off to prison, dude.

"Wow, at least you're honest," I replied sarcastically, but refused to return his phone calls.

He made his statement. And he had to live with the consequences.

Of course, there are men like Steve, who made it clear to me when he said, "Janice, I'm just not into relationships that are one-on-one. I won't marry anyone." You have to admire a man like Steve, who puts his cards on the table. I was upset when I heard the news, because it's every woman's fantasy to marry a handsome millionaire like him. But he wouldn't marry. He wouldn't even have a one-on-one relationship. In his case, it wasn't serial cheating—it was a lifestyle he defined for himself.

This isn't typical of most men.

Most guys pretend they're exclusive with you, and then start shopping elsewhere when you're not looking—or worse yet, when you *are* looking, but not really *seeing*.

Ask yourself: What do you want? Do you want a proud cheater?

Remind yourself: All men cheat. I don't give a rat's ass who they are. At one point, all men cheat (and so do women). A ring on your finger or his finger doesn't mean he's not cheating; it just means he's committing adultery.

Given all of this knowledge, it might seem logical to say that we simply have to put up with it and move on.

Bullshit. You don't have to put up with it if you don't want to.

It's more about the bond than it is about who's cheating. Once the bond is broken between the two of you, it's fucking broken. Call for the check.

WHAT TO DO WHEN YOU SEE YOUR GIRLFRIEND'S MAN CHEATING

Rat that motherfucker's ass out so fast it makes his head spin.

Like I said, people often cheat, and it's up to you to decide what's acceptable and what isn't. But why should anyone feel the need to cover for some guy who's dating your girlfriend?

Just tell your poor girlfriend, "Honey, please don't shoot the messenger, but I saw your new boyfriend out with that ratty-ass bitch who works at Nordstrom in the men's socks department. Investigate immediately."

At this point, she will either start screaming or start crying. Don't offer a lot of advice. You're just here to pass along some bad news that needs to be passed. You're Christiane Amanpour, not Oprah.

Sure, she'll end up interrogating you for all the dirty details, and you should be as specific as she is capable of hearing. Yes, you saw Ralph (don't call him names now) at Koi with the bitch, and yes, he was stroking her inner thigh while they did tequila shots. Yes, she was wearing what looked like a nightgown. Yes, you saw them macking. Yes, tongues were seen in the area. No, Ralph didn't really see you, because he was too busy figuring out how to have an orgasm in a public place without being arrested.

Listen to your girlfriend scream, yell, and cry. Agree that he's a no-good prick with no dick who doesn't deserve her. (At least you're telling the truth.) Don't launch into a tirade about how you always knew Ralph was worthless. She knows all of the above from living with him and doesn't need you to remind her. Don't get involved in a bashfest. This could come back to haunt you if she forgives him for his cheating or if he lies to her and insists that you were on drugs and he was out saving the whales that night.

After passing on the news, you just need to hang up and realize that in the morning she's going to hate you more than she hates him. You're the one who ratted the bastard out, but he's *her* rat bastard. If only you didn't pass on this message, she wouldn't know.

It's not you who's sticking it to that little man-thief, but it might as well be you. She might eventually forgive you—or not. You're still in the right for ratting him out.

First of all, it's worth it not to have that weight on your chest. I don't care if you could hide it for a few weeks, it would tug on you until you couldn't stand it anymore. You might tell interested third parties and then it would get back to her. She'd hate you more for passing it around and not telling her, and she'd have a point there.

Lesson 42

It Happens to the Best of Us

THE ORACLE GETS DUMPED

It would be very romance-novelistic to end this book by telling you that Timothy and I declared our true love and joined each other at a peak time for both of us: our sexual primes.

That would be fiction, and this book is 100 percent fact.

I helped Timothy with some shopping and helped him explore career opportunities. I listened while he talked about his family and his future, carefully not pushing to see if I had a spot in his next chapter. One night, I even saved his life—and this has nothing to do with sex.

One night, after sex, I woke up to find him passed out on my bathroom floor. Cold. Out.

It was one of the scariest sights ever. After I determined that he had a pulse, I frantically dialed 911. Wondering if he'd had a heart attack, or an epileptic fit, or who knows what, I pressed towels soaked in cold water to his head until finally he showed signs of life. Then I heard the blare of an ambulance roaring down the street.

"Janice, I forgot to tell you," he said when he awoke. "I'm prone to fainting spells." He was slowly riding the wave back into consciousness.

"Oh, baby," I said, while thinking, "Oh, shit. What's going to happen next?"

Silly question. Obviously *next* came in the form of a joyride to Cedars-Sinai, where I called my fabulous internist and told him to run every test in the book. Of course, I took complete charge of the entire hospital, making sure his every need was taken care of. (Except a certain nurse fantasy, which I informed Timothy should wait until he wasn't feeling quite so light-headed—I wasn't sure if insurance would cover the aftermath of the Big Dog.)

After the shopping, the counseling, the love, the sex, the medical advice, the promise of great future sex, the being nice to his family, the being there for his every emotional twist and turn, Timothy did what every woman in America has come to expect from a man these days.

Did he pop the question?

Wake up! Now *you're* getting light-headed on me. No, he disappeared from sight. For a week. Just up and left. No phone call. No explanation. No word.

I broke my own rules and called his cell. His message came on immediately, so I hung up. It's old-fashioned, but the only acceptable response. I don't like leaving messages, I like making impressions.

I knew I should call for the check. But I hesitated.

A week later, Timothy called me. He said he was in Ohio. On business. Very busy. Meetings. Thought about me all the time.

"I didn't know about the hardships they have in Ohio," I said coldly.

He said, "Uh, what hardships?"

Me: "Obviously, they don't have phone service."

As we talked, reality set in: Timothy was calling the check on me. I was going to do it, but I'd held back. And so, instead, the Oracle had been officially dumped.

I hung up on him, but not before I told him to listen to me the next morning on the Jamie and Danny radio show in Los Angeles, which is the hot morning-drive talk show on Star 98.7, hosted by Jamie White and Danny Bonaduce of *Partridge Family* infamy. Naturally, they wanted me to come on and talk about men. I figured I could use my latest radio interview as a Help Wanted for a new boyfriend—and possibly infuriate an old, in-the-doghouse, ex-boyfriend into seeing the light at the same time.

"You guys need tips on finding men?" I asked the listeners the next day.

"Are you looking for a man?" Danny asked me.

"Oh, I'm *looking*," I said with gusto, hoping Timothy was in bed, alone, listening to the early-morning banter.

I had to take callers on the show. A woman called up to ask me what I want in a man. It's a great, simple question, and I decided not to think about the answer. I just let it flow from the depths of my heart.

"I need a man who lets me be myself," I began. "One who's not trying to change, control, or override me. I don't need a man who wants to tell me when not to speak or how to behave. I don't want a man telling me what fork to use or how much cash should be in my bank account."

Then a lightbulb went off in my brain.

"I need a man who realizes that I'm okay just the way he found me. In fact, *all* of us girls are better than okay," I said. "Our imperfections are what make us human, and how dare anyone do a makeover on what's inside?"

The girl on the phone line didn't get it. She went on to say that she was planning to join a gym. Wanted to drop twenty pounds. Thought this would lead to romantic bliss. That it would lead to a healthier, slimmer body. But she clearly wasn't understanding the important stuff—that all that sweatin' to the oldies would just bring her into contact with more men and present more opportunities for her to get her heart snapped in two.

"When you're at the gym, remember—you're doing that for yourself," I said. "You're not there to make your man happy."

"I just want to get laid," the girl said.

If only it were that simple. It's a fine line between the Oracle and the Orifice.

That day, I headed home a little depressed because there was no man waiting for me at my house. Here I was writing a book about dating, mating, and extricating—and that fucking extricating part was rearing its ugly head again. You know how all of us get in those moods? We're never going to find love again? We're going to be single until we turn old and die in our sleep? About three smelly months later, someone will find the bones? That was me.

Just when I'd decided I was heading to Spinsterville, I heard a beautiful sound—and it wasn't my cell phone ringing.

It was a loud wolf whistle. From the construction guy working on a roof across the street.

A few seconds of despair, and one whistle later I was back in business. I was feeling my sexy self again. I started wondering: Could a supermodel and a construction worker ever find true love, or should we settle for just hot sex? Because I was pretty sure it would be at least hot sex. Would he try to change me? Would he expect me to wash those dirty clothes? But oh, those big, calloused hands! Sounded like a good VH1 show.

I decided to jump back in the car and drive out to Malibu all by myself. It was eighty perfect degrees outside and all the men were walking around shirtless. I did a little people-watching and enjoyed the warm sunshine on my face. For an entire afternoon, I didn't date, mate, or extricate. I took some time to myself to celebrate.

Remember, you can be your own best company.

But what about that bare-chested guy walking on the beach? Hold that thought.

ROYALLY SCREWED

If we're talking about being dumped, we have to talk about my date with Dodi al-Fayed, right before he started dating Princess Di.

My sister Debbie was dating Mohammed Khashoggi, who happens to be Dodi's cousin. Somehow, Dodi got my number, and through the years I received occasional calls from him: "Meet me on St. Barts."

"Meet me in Monaco." "Meet me in Tokyo." He must've seen an English *Vogue* cover or two.

I agreed to have dinner with him at Beau Rivage in Malibu, an out-of-the-way place. It was a blind date, and I have to say the man had charm.

As a dinner present for me for accepting the date I'd put off for years, Dodi brought me a platinum Cartier tank watch encrusted with diamonds; I'm sure he was thinking I was gonna fuck him later, which I didn't. By the end of the dessert, all I was thinking about was the matching earrings.

The next thing I knew, he was dating Di. I left him a message saying "Well, what about me?" He didn't call back—he'd already called the check on me.

I couldn't compete with royalty. I'm glad, or I could've been in that limo on the way to the airport.

DUMPED, THE DAY AFTER

It never fails: The day after you've been dumped is the day you decide the man who dumped you was the love of your life. You're sure there will never be another man who will love you. You're sure this was the best sex of your life. This might have been the last sex of your life.

None of the above is true, but you're allowed to wallow in the angst if it's the day or even week after the dump. We're only human.

One coping strategy is to surround yourself with gay men. They're even better than girlfriends when it comes to dissing the fucker who dumped you. They've been there, too, and know the dump makes you feel so raw that you're almost bleeding inside.

You can also find moments *not* to talk about the dump with your gay male friends. They'll suddenly lure you into a conversation about fashion, and before you know it you're actually agreeing that Gautier this season was better than Dolce & Gabbana, but Thierry Mugler is *always* great. It's called fashion therapy, and it works.

I've always taken consolation in thinking about other famous dump victims, and that's why I'm lucky to live in Los Angeles, where half the population's love life is chronicled in *Us Weekly*. Once, I got The Call while I was at my gym and suddenly my eyes fixed on a pair of dark and very toned calf muscles. As my eyes traveled up her body, I prayed it was a certain icon, but was afraid I couldn't handle another disappointment. But there she was—Diana Ross! I could've kissed the ground at her feet. She was inquiring about membership at the Equinox Gym in the Sunset Plaza, but I felt she was sent to give me the strength to stand there and listen to a man tell me he couldn't see me anymore.

Ain't no mountain high enough! my mind screamed. *Ain't no valley low enough!* I had no time to grieve. Diana Ross is better than Prozac.

And don't forget, she's also available in convenient CD form.

ROAD TO RECOVERY

When you've been dumped, it's very likely the asshole will call you a few days later and leave you a variation on this fucking phone message: "Listen, I just wanted to call to check on how you're doing."

They always do this to you. It's in their genes. Just when you're feeling one measly percent better about yourself, they try to suck you back into the dark hole of life without them. They don't care if you've killed yourself. Actually, they do care, just in case one day in the distant future they might want to consider calling you to see if you'll fuck them again. But they're not genuinely concerned with your mental health.

Never call him back. It's the same premise that I used years ago to fend off my father, the pedophile. You must be strong. You can't ever give in. You can't let him win.

"This is evil," one gay friend of mine said after coming over to listen to one such message I received after a dump. "He's calling to make sure you're alive. He's calling to make you think he's not a total scum-sucking bastard, because he thinks to call after dumping a woman. But that just makes him even more of a scum-sucking bastard."

Don't call him back. What do you do instead, when you're ready to recover?

Throw yourself into the gym. For *you*, remember? Not for him, or the next him.

Jump into beauty activities.

Focus on service work. I mean it. Volunteer for the homeless. Pick up trash by public schools. Work at a soup kitchen. Paint that dotted yellow line down the center of the highway. You'll save the world while feeling better about your own life.

And surround yourself with friends.

And, when you're ready, you can always try the hair of the dog—in the form of a little harmless flirtation with someone new. It's a great way to get over a broken heart. Revenge isn't about staying at home sulking—revenge is being at the par-tay.

Lesson 43

Extricate Now! Ask Me How

HOW TO DUMP A GUY IN TEN SECONDS FLAT

It's always hard to end things with a mate, unless he's a total prick and that's why you're doing it. In that case, you can just say, 'It's off. Don't call me again." I've done that.

But when it's someone you still care about, it's tough. When I'm faced with a man like that, I tell him, "The balance is off." It's true, but it's nonspecific. It's something they can't dispute. If you feel the balance is off, it's off. I think it's a great line—it's the new, "It's not you, it's me."

The one time when you've really got to take extra care in ending it is when you're cohabiting. Trying to get him out of the house can be a delicate proposition. I told one live-in who I was trying to move out that I was trying to kick my coffee addiction.

I know, I know. But it worked.

TOP TEN DEALBREAKERS

(10) WHEN IT'S ALL ABOUT THE MONEY—AND *NOTHING BUT* THE MONEY. All winking and kidding aside, if you get into a relationship *only* for money, you're a penny-nickel-dime-quarter slut. And whatever you do, you should *never* marry for money. Look at these

bitches in Brentwood or Bel-Air—the drop-dead gorgeous ones with ugly, rich husbands. They all know who they are, and they know, in their constricted little hearts, that they got hitched for the cash. Only if you're totally soulless and mindless can you be happy with that arrangement.

As I've said, I did it myself once. I married the king of trolls. Wasn't worth it.

And this palm-lined boulevard goes both ways, too. Anyone who hooks up with *you* for money should be dispensed with pronto. How can you tell? Because he'll know more about your finances than you do—and he'll always find a way to be in the men's room when the check arrives. First time that happens, have *your* check waiting for him when he returns.

(9) WHEN SOMETHING SMELLS FISHY. If they don't smell good, forget it. Their pH level and saliva must be perfect; if he thinks his spit doesn't stink and it does, bye-bye. You may think this is petty, but it's not: The fact is, we humans are attracted or repelled on a chemical level, and there's no use trying to fight it.

I knew one guy who went out with a girlfriend of mine and, to put it politely, he stunk like a skunk. She was a hot supermodel, and she was actually considering getting a pair of nose plugs, just to tolerate the stench! I gave her the answer in one word: Check!

I also know a very handsome Greek man who dated a woman who was gorgeous, but he couldn't go down on her. He didn't have a hang-up about oral sex, he said; it was just that she smelled foul. He called me and asked, "Do you think I can tell her to bathe?" My response? "Call for the check. Skanky is as skanky does." This guy is great looking, and he's supposed to walk around wondering if his face smells like oysters in the sun after sex? Personally, I believe everyone should get in a tub before sex. That's why Japanese men rule. They must take forty baths a day.

(8) WHEN ABSENCE DOESN'T MAKE THE HEART GROW FONDER. Long-distance relationships don't work. Why? Sit back and let me tell you a story.

One evening a few years back, I attended a *Vogue* party at the Louvre. I was wearing couture Versace, with a fake ponytail slicked back down to my butt. Earlier that very day, Sly Stallone and I had given each other the boot. I might have spent weeks mourning my breakup with an A-list actor who I once thought was the father of my baby, but it was over with Sly that morning and by that evening I was out with a new man—Ron Galotti, the publisher of American *Vogue*. Now that's timing!

I was being put up at the Ritz in Paris for the Versace show. That night, after the party, the publisher walked me home. We walked all over the city, Ron in his tux and me in my seven-inch stiletto heels, until seven in the morning. "He isn't the one," I told myself, "but he is *Vogue*."

But it's hard to turn one night in Paris into a permanent romance. Ron and I began a long-distance relationship between New York and L.A., and it worked for a heartbeat. But only for a heartbeat. Separation leads to anxiety leads to permanent separation. Not long after, he started dating that thin-lipped, no-talent Candace Bushnell—he was the original Mr. Big in *Sex and the City*. If I'd known that Ronnie baby could have helped me get published, I could forgive you for thinking that was why I was with him. But no, I wasn't even writing at that point. I wasn't that smart.

Long-distance affairs work for only two kinds of people: flight attendants and people who don't have sex together anymore.

(7) WHEN SOMEBODY FORGETS HIS MANNERS. If they eat like pigs, fart a lot, or swear like truckers, then they just have bad manners. And bad manners will put a damper on anyone's positive energy flow.

(6) WHEN FAMILY VALUES AMOUNT TO FAMILY BULLSHIT. If yours doesn't like him and/or his doesn't like you, that's bound to make for a toxic journey. Marry the man and you're marrying the family, like it or not. I understand this firsthand, having married and divorced several families myself. And now that I have my own family, if a chick I don't like for my son comes along, I guarantee you I'll snuff the bitch. The Big Dog is all bark *and* all bite.

(5) WHEN HE WON'T GET TESTED. Don't kid yourself: We're still in the AIDS crisis. Just last week, someone near and dear to me found out he was HIV-positive. It reminds me—and should remind you—that your partners need to be tested. Don't show me the money. Show me your AIDS test.

(4) WHEN HE CAN'T STOP TRYING TO CONTROL YOU. Forget about it. Nobody deserves to be controlled like a dog on a leash. Your love partner should want to roll *with* you, not *over* you. He should want you to be *you*—the vibing, rolling, laughing, snapping, happy *you*. He shouldn't argue with the real you or try to change you. The right man will not only accept you, but enjoy you, as you are. Only an insecure person wants total control. And remember that this mirror has two faces.

(3) WHEN HIS CHEATING HEART STARTS BEATING. It's *verboten.* That said, I also know that, at one time or another, all men and most women cheat. I've never met anyone who hasn't cheated.

Which is why, in my book, there are second chances—because people can slip up. If you truly love your man, you'll give him a second chance. But it's up to you to find your own breaking point.

Mine is when the other person thinks of cheating as a hobby.

(2) WHEN HE'S MEAN TO YOUR KIDS. There are no second chances here! Quick story: When my son was seven years old, a man I was dating smacked him. Here was my sweet son fumbling around with this man's suitcase at the Maui airport and this adult man, who'd had one too many red wines in the airport bar, backhanded him so hard that he fell down on the concrete and started crying. The minute I saw this happen, I ran over and said, "It's over, you asshole." I dumped him on the fucking spot. He hit my kid, so he hit the bricks. I don't care if he offered me a million-dollar deal, that was it: You don't hit my kids. I should have sued the guy, but didn't because I hate our lawsuit-happy society. But if they're abusive in any way, call for the check—and then the cops.

(1) WHEN THE SEX AIN'T DOING IT FOR YOU. Bad sex? Goodbye. If it starts out bad, it'll never get better. In fact, sex only gets worse over time, but by then, with luck, you'll have other consolations— friendship, humor, a MINI Cooper.

Think of it this way: Sex with a new man is like a bouquet of flowers—it's gorgeous, but it fades steadily until it dries up and you get rid of it. So if someone handed you a bouquet of dead flowers, would you put them in water?

BONUS DEALBREAKER

Closet cases. If you find your man in your closet trying on your clothes, then it's over. I'm speaking from experience. One night, a guy came out of my closet/temple wearing my red La Perla lingerie. This guy was six foot four—and that lingerie is *way* too expensive for some big hairy guy to stretch it out! There is no room to grow in my G string.

Nothing against all my transvestite friends, but when it comes to getting my own groove on, I can't take men dressed as women seriously. Once you've made out with Gia, a dude in panties is a big step down.

Lesson 44

Don't Swear Off Men or Oxygen !

THE BABY'S FATE IN THE WAKE OF THE BATHWATER

I once went on a date with a man named Tom, a beautiful, sweet guy who works at MTV, where I sometimes do VH1 shows like *40 Most Awesomely Bad Dirrty Songs . . . Ever* and *I Love the '90s: Part Deux* for them. We had a nice time (read: not exciting, no sex, pleasant conversation) on our first date, and he asked me out again. The only problem was, I was just getting out of a relationship with a CEO of an electronics conglomerate. Part of me didn't want to have a great time with Tom on our first date because I was sure I'd be calling the check on him someday in the future. Why? Because even though he's nice, he's still a man.

On our second date, I was in rare form. I couldn't stop myself; I just kept saying horrible things to Tom, one after another.

Me: "Do you think you'll ever really make your movie, or are you one of those guys who's been working on something for twenty years?"

Me: "Is that your real hair?"

Me (to myself): "Why am I being such a bitch?"

When he dropped me off in total silence later that night, I called a girlfriend and we talked about how it is that women can be so mean.

"Life is just a series of really horrible things that happen to you," said my girlfriend. "Sometimes it just builds up, and you need to take it out on someone,"

"Tom did look at me like, 'What the fuck's wrong with you?' " I told her. "Men. That's what's wrong with me."

I mean, come on—I'd just destroyed the beginning of what could have been a nice thing with Tom. The clincher was in his car when I began to tell him about my fucked-up CEO boyfriend, who was screwing half of Los Angeles behind my back. A sweet man to the end, Tom listened and pretended that he cared, but there was smoke coming from his tires when he peeled out of my driveway at maximum speed that night.

Later that night, I tried to call Tom and apologize. He was very nice about it, and suggested that anyone could have a bad night. (What about a bad decade?) Tom even suggested a third date, which I accepted with half a heart. We made plans for that Sunday, and he called on Saturday to confirm. He was up for Round Three with the Big Dog, a.k.a. the Giant Bitch. My question: Why?

"What's the matter with this guy?" I thought. "How could he still want to go out with me?"

A little while later, I canceled the date. Tom was not a do-over type of man. He'd already been done over by me. He'd already seen my worst side and I didn't want to take him there again. In a way, I was proud of myself for putting his feelings first in this case.

He called me a bunch of times in the days and weeks that followed, but I never picked up. I could already see myself dating Tom a few times and then saying, "Okay, let's take a break."

After a breakup, sometimes it's best to just lay low and admit to yourself, *I don't want to be dating right now—and to hell with an actual relationship*. A few months later, when I was in a better place, I tried to e-mail Tom and apologize again. "If you ever want to get together again for lunch," I wrote, "with no strings . . . call me."

He never did. Tom knew I wasn't ready, and he'd called the check on me. It was the right move.

A few weeks after this little drama, I met Peter, a fellow model, a twenty-eight-year-old hottie with blond hair gelled straight back. I decided to go out with him for one good reason: He's tall, and I know how to wear heels. That's right—sometimes dating is nothing more than a way to give your best shoes a chance to show you what they can do.

Peter is unlike other men in that it doesn't freak him out when I ask him to dinner. He doesn't need to be in complete control of our budding "relationship," because there is none. I just want to make out with this guy, and he's willing. It gets me over the CEO like nothing else can.

If you want to go into hibernation, that's fine—whether it's in your bedroom or some nice upscale boutique. But don't swear off men forever, because you'll make yourself a liar sooner than you can imagine.

Sisters Can Do It for Themselves

NO MAN'S LAND

I think Angelina Jolie has the right idea. She's after contentment, which is what this book is about. And her brand of contentment is not necessarily about walking down the aisle.

Sure, I'd like to get married again someday and maybe even adopt.

Do I need a man to adopt a child? Again, Angelina has the right idea. She has the children, but she doesn't have the man around telling her she's too old or that her language is too abrasive or that she's too emotional during that time of the month. (I'd love for all men to get a period just once and try to contain their emotions. I'd pay money to see it.)

Angelina is content. She's also self-sufficient without a man. She can pay for Maddox's and Zahara's great-grandchildren's private education. Her earning power beats out any guy's I've ever met. Even Brad is not a requirement—he's a check waiting to happen.

Maybe I should hook up with Angelina.

Honey, if you're reading this, give Janice a call.

I'd take you over Eminem.

Special Advice for Brad and Jen (Because I Care!)

The entire planet mourned when Brad Pitt and Jennifer Aniston decided to call the check on each other last year. What is the matter with these superstars? Why didn't they just consult me for dating advice?

What follows is my love-extra for Jen because she can make the moves to get him back even in the face of stiff competition from Angelina. This advice is easy to adapt to your own life, too, even if you're hardly Jennifer Aniston and your boyfriend ain't Brad Pitt by any stretch.

ADVICE FROM THE BIG DOG TO THE FORMER FRIEND:

(1) SPEND MORE TIME WITH HIM. Whatever happened to "I'll be there for you?" I mean, would you leave Brad Pitt alone? You can't leave guys like that to their own devices because they'll figure out ways to share their devices with other women.

(2) DON'T PUT YOUR CAREER SO FAR AHEAD OF YOUR MARRIAGE. Do you really need to work? Don't you have enough money? I'm single. I'll take some of your acting roles to let you spend more time with Brad.

(3) TART YOURSELF UP A BIT. That hippie look is *soooo* over. Go couture! Have some really erotic photos of yourself taken for Brad—then drop those bad boys off at his doorstep. What do you think Angelina was doing with that *W* spread?

(4) HAVE A SHOWDOWN WITH ANGELINA. Hell, you and Angelina ought to have an affair! You'd be a hot couple.

(5) AND IF ALL ELSE FAILS . . . Go throw yourself at Colin Farrell.

The End Is Not Always the ~~End~~

SIGNS OF LIFE

There was a woman standing in the rubble by the side of the road on Sunset Boulevard. She was holding a huge cardboard sign with black ink letters all over it: "Got robbed. Need help. Child needs dental work. Please give."

The night before, a man had walked by me at the gym with eyes the color of the Mediterranean. I'd walked on by, looking beyond the eyes that should have knocked me off my feet.

"Janice, what's up with that?" I thought, forcing myself to turn around and approach him.

"Aren't you an actor?" I asked him.

"Well, I used to do soaps," he replied with a smile that could melt steel.

"Well . . . you're hot," I retorted. Under the circumstances it was the best I had in me.

He ended up asking me out for dinner. It turned out the beautiful man with the great eyes happened to co-own a hot restaurant with Ashton Kutcher.

"Want to meet me there at eight?" he asked me.

Now my heart, still bruised from recent disappointments, betrayed me. "I don't go out much," I lied.

"I'll have a limo pick you up," he insisted. But I blew off the limo that night because I just was not ready. I just sat at home and consoled myself with the evidence that I've still got it.

Oh, all right—I sat home dwelling on the old-news fact that I'd been dumped.

The next day, I encountered that woman with the sign. Moments before I saw her, I'd been walking around in my little post-break-up zone, sad and depressed, wondering why I'd given up a chance at a nice, fun date with a boy with Mediterranean-blue eyes. But seeing her with her sign helped me decide to accept my chaotic life. With this book in development, my ongoing TV prospects, a lovely home, my two great kids—all of that in reverse order—my life, I realized, was pretty damn good.

I actually stopped and talked to her for a minute to reinforce the idea that life is not just about men. It's about many other things, including helping other women. I offered to help her get a line on a job, and she seemed grateful. After all, no woman should have to stand in the gravel and beg.

It's the same thing with relationships. Don't wind up in the gravel begging.

Although, now that I think of it, the idea of holding up a sign is interesting.

Maybe I'll make one of my own: "Got dumped. Bring on a billionaire with a big . . . heart!"

A GAME OF TWENTY QUESTIONS FOR THE ORACLE

While I was writing this book, I decided to take a few questions from rank-and-file daters, maters, and extricaters. Lots of stuff I couldn't fit in anywhere else.

And unlike, say, motocross racing naked, this is something I recommend you do try at home. Make a date with a good girlfriend, fire up some popcorn, and interview each other about your love lives. I guarantee you'll surprise her—and yourself.

Q: Are you really a diva?
Janice: I go to bed with my high heels on. What do you think?

Q: What do you do with a jealous man?
Janice: Make him *more* jealous.

Q: Do you believe in astrology?
Janice: Absolutely. But I don't adhere to it.

Q: What do all men want in bed?
Janice: I don't want to do the tragic slut thing. This book isn't like that. But oh, my God—blow jobs and tongue up the butt.

Q: If you sleep around, does that automatically make you a slut?
Janice: I don't view myself as a slut. I view myself as a modern woman.

Q: Have you ever sworn off guys completely?
Janice: Every day. It's like trying to stop drinking coffee. I can't do it. I fall in love every time a leaf falls off a tree, and by the time it hits the ground I'm over it.

Q: What's the difference between older men and younger guys?
Janice: Thickness of wallet.

Q: Is there any dirty talk that mandates calling for the check?
Janice: I've gotten, "I had sex this morning thinking of you, baby." I also once flirtatiously asked a man what his favorite porno was, and he said, "Actually, I saw a porn where the guy was doing the girl and, like, shoving her head in the toilet. It was cool." These might be good examples.

Q: Do you believe in love at first sight?

Janice: After a while, you've got to—when, say, the sushi chef starts looking good. I do believe in the possibility of love at first sight. But I also believe in temporary insanity.

Q: Who are the best men to date?

Janice: Gay men, Jews, and me. We're the best. I like men who have polish. Wit. A sense of flair. A sense of cents.

Q: Are you *sure* you don't believe long-distance relationships can work? What if the guy is way hot?

Janice: I don't think they work. I know *I* can't do the long-distance-love-affair thing. I don't know how people do West Coast/East Coast things. It's hard enough when they live down the block.

Q: What's a good way to get a man's attention if you're in public and he's with another woman?

Janice: Wear a little-girl skirt and flash him. He'll take notice. Or talk loudly about the fourteen-hour blow job you're famous for. This works! I did this in the lobby of the Royalton in New York and a married man became so distracted he bit his finger thinking it was a deep-fried green olive.

Q: Is it okay for a man or a woman to bring a friend along on a date?

Janice: Unless the friend is Bill Gates or Oprah, stay home. Unless the friend has a Lear jet, he or she cannot possibly add anything to the date and he or she cannot possibly *not* detract from it.

Q: You seem to take your children's well-being very seriously. Have they ever been caught in the crossfire during a dating drama?

Janice: Children are not stupid. They know if Mom is happy and in love or stressed and in the dumps. Nobody's perfect, and there are going to be times when they see or hear more than you want them to.

When I got dumped to the curb after the Golden Globes, I called my date up screaming, "You've got a fucking screw loose! You're fucking gay if you don't wanna be with me!" My children heard my tantrum, though, and they realized that this was some kind of heartbreaking situation for me. They were like, "Mom . . . are you okay?"

After that, I've made sure they'll never hear any of that again. You have to protect them and let them be children.

Q: I know what you're saying about married and separated men, but this guy I'm hot for is two seconds from his divorce being final. What about that situation?
Janice: When a separated man who wants you insists he's two seconds away from a divorce, tell him, "Call me in two seconds."

Q: What's the most important thing to keep in mind if you're going to have an affair?
Janice: Make best friends with the concierge. I recommend the Royalton. And when it ends—and it will!—make sure you're packed in advance so you can leave quickly and with dignity. Never let them see the waterworks.

Q: What's the nicest thing a guy's ever done for you?
Janice: I'm tempted to say "fucked my lights out." But I think the nicest thing is just being there to listen to me when I'm going through a crisis.

Not that it happens every day, guys. Just from time to time.

Q: Do you ever worry about coming on too strong?
Janice: Never! Do what you love, and if that means coming out swinging, that's what's going to happen. I'm doing what I love—dating men and then writing about it. I really am America's sweetheart. It's about time for America to realize it. Fuck Katie Couric. She just broke up with

that billionaire Tom Warner—maybe I *should* fuck Katie Couric. Or if he's a billionaire, maybe I should fuck *him!*

So back to the question—wait, you think I come on too strong?

Q: How do you keep a man on his toes?
Janice: Whenever flowers are delivered anywhere nearby, always pretend they're for you. Send yourself a bouquet and leave it around the house for him to see. Flowers have recycling uses, too. I like to remove the petals from roses and stick them in my panties before a date if the guy has a good sense of humor. We'll be engrossed in conversation and I'll say, "Hey, wait—what's this?" and reach into my skirt and remove the petals, blowing them all over his face. Believe me, it creates quite an impression.

If he laughs, he's a good guy. If he gets incredibly horny, he's a great guy. If he acts like you're insane, he's just boring and you need to call for the check.

That's how I keep a man on his toes—I keep surprising him, testing him, keep him guessing.

If you just want to know how to keep a man eager for your date that night, end your final call before the date with, "You may get the ass tonight." Then snap the cell phone shut. It seems to be a winner. It also ensures he won't be tardy.

Q: You have books' worth of wisdom, but do you have a creed?
Janice: Yeah: Play real hard, fuck real hard, work real hard, and live your goddamn life being as real as you can be—because it's over real fast.

END RUN—JANICE DICKINSON WILL NEVER GO QUIETLY

I once read an article about me with the headline "Janice Dickinson Will Never Go Quietly." Now, that made me laugh—I loved it. I will not come quietly, either.

I didn't want to end this book without a little more juice and a little more substance, so I have some parting thoughts. I always have to have the last word, which is only fair—fuck if it isn't my own book.

Remember: Never hold back.

Don't Follow Trends— Start Them

FOLLOWING YOUR HEART

The more things I find out about men, the less I understand them.

All of us ladies are in the same situation. For instance, the other morning I got a call from a gorgeous, tall, independent nurse friend of mine.

"Janice, help me," she cried. "I want to get a guy. Quick!"

"We don't get guys quick," I reminded her.

"Can't I just use *The Rules?*" she asked.

"*The Rules* are bullshit," I said. "They don't work. Didn't one of those chicks get divorced right after the book came out?"

"Aren't we supposed to be demure and wait for the guy to act?" my girlfriend asked.

"You can demure yourself right out of the ballpark," I told her. "Take charge. Follow your heart."

"How far should I follow my heart?" she asked me. And I had an epiphany.

"I haven't reached that point on the map yet."

MR. RIGHT ISN'T A MAN

My son, Nathan, graduated from high school recently, and on that day something profound happened to me. When I saw him across the auditorium in his cap, he really became my one and true and only. I was so fuckin' proud of him, I can't even tell you. I wasn't even crying, though I bawl every time I tell this story. I was just filled with welled-up, pent-up pride.

I was numb for the rest of the day. But it all came out that night. My daughter, Savvy, kept wanting to be the center of attention. I just turned to her and said, "Honey, this moment is important to me. One day I'll have the same kind of moment with you. For now, I need you to behave." She was cool with that. Like I say, they don't call her Savvy for nothing.

Nathan ignored me the whole day, but finally he looked over my way. He must have know I was dying—I'm never that quiet. Gone was his usual nemesis Stalker Mom, pumping her fist in front of his friends and shouting, "Hey, Nathan! What's up? Yeah!" Now? Nothing but silence.

He gave me one shot out of the corner of his eye, as if to say, "Uh-huh, you're all right." And, my God. I just exhaled eighteen years of memories. Oh, it was so wonderful! So amazing. Un. Fucking. Believable. Inexplicable.

What I realized, in that moment, was that I don't truly need any man—just my kids. Without that need, I can continue to be fabulous and me, and the rest doesn't matter.

Yeah, the feeling of having a guy wake up next to you is great, but how long will it last? You can't know. Parenthood is forever.

I felt like I was graduating that day, too.

THE BOTTOM LINE

As women, we're prone to becoming so overwhelmed with romance—with the heat, the pheromones, and the passion. We meet someone new, and in a flash we've lost our psychic selves. We walk in the shadows. I see these shadow walkers all over Beverly Hills, New York City, Tokyo, Sydney—everywhere! Put your life in the hands of a man, and he'll take over every time.

Men use their power over women. Give yourself over to a man, and suddenly you can find yourself with nothing to say—or, worse yet, with no say at all over the way your life is unfolding.

Stop.

You have the power to date, mate, and extricate. You have the power to refuse to tolerate physical or emotional abuse. You have the right to dismiss anything or anyone who lowers your dignity or chips away at your self-esteem. You even have the power to remove yourself from the whole cycle and focus on you, unencumbered by a male accessory.

Don't let anyone bring you down. Remember everything the Oracle told you. And keep rockin'.

Drop me a note about all the ways you've called for the check—or have decided not to call for the check.

I'll make a few notes myself and get back to you soon . . . in the next book.

INDEX